GARDEN WILDLIFE

Revealing Your
Garden's Secrets

GARDEN WILDLIFE

Revealing Your Garden's Secrets

GERARD E CHESHIRE

WHITE OWL

First published in Great Britain in 2019 by
PEN & SWORD WHITE OWL
An imprint of
Pen & Sword Books Ltd
Yorkshire - Philadelphia

Copyright © Gerard E Cheshire

Hardback ISBN 9781526729699
Paperback ISBN 9781526751522

Printed and bound by Replika Press Pvt. Ltd.
Design: Pen & Sword - Paul Wilkinson

Pen & Sword Books Ltd incorporates the Imprints of Aviation, Atlas,
Family History, Fiction, Maritime, Military, Discovery, Politics, History,
Archaeology, Select, Wharncliffe Local History, Wharncliffe True Crime,
Military Classics, Wharncliffe Transport, Leo Cooper, The Praetorian Press,
Remember When, Seaforth Publishing and Frontline Publishing.
For a complete list of Pen & Sword titles please contact

PEN & SWORD BOOKS LTD
47 Church Street, Barnsley, South Yorkshire, S70 2AS, England
E-mail: enquiries@pen-and-sword.co.uk
Website: www.pen-and-sword.co.uk

Or
PEN AND SWORD BOOKS
1950 Lawrence Rd, Havertown, PA 19083, USA
E-mail: Uspen-and-sword@casematepublishers.com
Website: www.penandswordbooks.com

CONTENTS

Painted Lady Butterfly.

Helen M Bushe

INTRODUCTION

The aim of this book is to encourage the reader to think about their garden in a new way. We have long been used to the idea that a garden should be a manicured, kempt and ordered space, almost as if it were an external room. As a result, many gardens have become unnatural and sterile even though they may have lawns, shrubs and flowerbeds in abundance. This is because lawns and flowerbeds are frequently free of the self-seeded plants we often call weeds. In addition, the majority of garden plants are non-indigenous species and cultivars that offer nothing to our indigenous wildlife. Furthermore, gardens are kept so tidy that there are few compost heaps, log piles and overgrown corners in which animals can make their homes and forage for food.

Therefore, the 'new way' of looking at our gardens is simply to reject this nonsense and accept a return to the 'old way' of looking at our gardens, as natural and wild spaces, rather than unnatural and tame spaces. To let them get a bit untidy and to allow nature to reclaim them; to stop using weed killers and bug sprays and to allow our indigenous plants and creatures to reinvade our green spaces; to begin thinking of our gardens as a network of habitats that allow and encourage our wildlife to continue living alongside us, even in the housing estates that steadily spread as the mark of modern suburbia.

As this book is about wildlife found in gardens, then it focuses on those species that are most likely to be seen in typical gardens, rather than providing comprehensive coverage of all species, as many species are seldom seen in gardens, unless those gardens happen to be in unusual localities. The idea of a garden safari is to consider a typical garden in terms of the different habitats it offers from one corner to another, in much the same way that a real safari moves from habitat to habitat.

So, we have lawns that equate to meadow and grassland, we have ponds that equate to wetland and marshland, we have paths, patios and drives that equate to exposed bedrock, we have the hedgerows that equate to woodland, we have flower beds and vegetable patches that equate to forest clearings, we have walls that equate to cliff faces, we have roofs that equate to escarpments, we have rockeries that equate to plateaux, we have the forgotten corners, which equate to undergrowth and thicket, and we have sheds, garages and summerhouses that equate to caves, voids and hollows. Thus, within a typical garden there is usually quite a range of habitats from the point of view of wild plants and animals, even if we don't readily see it ourselves.

In fact, this inadvertent division of our gardens into many small habitats can mean that they offer sanctuary to a greater variety of species than might have been present in the landscape before the land was developed. When we put them all together, they offer a vast patchwork and network of small habitats that enable whole populations of many species to survive and flourish alongside us. All we need to do is be a bit more carefree about what the neighbours think, so that those habitats can come into their own.

Perhaps the best way to appreciate the way our wildlife views our gardens is to think about scale. Most plants and animals are a good deal smaller than we are, so they don't need that much space in order to make garden habitats their homes. Those that do require more space simply treat our gardens as a collective habitat, so they ignore our concept of boundaries and move about as they choose, on the ground, through the foliage or in the air. The notion of delineated land ownership is largely a peculiarity of humanity, although some species are territorial in order to maintain sufficient resources for their survival and reproduction. Many garden animals are diurnal (active by day), while others are crepuscular or nocturnal (active at twilight or by night). So, there are likely to be many more species living in our gardens than we immediately realize. In addition, the time of year can affect our observation of different species. Many sedentary species hibernate during the colder months, while others remain active. There are also migratory species, some of which depart for the colder months, while others arrive for the colder months. The life cycles of many species also dictate the way we see them during the seasons, as most breed annually, so the young and adult stages will appear at different times of the year. Of course, many animals hide from predators or secrete themselves in dark and damp places to avoid drying out. This often means that they live under objects close to the ground, or they live below the surface in cavities, holes and burrows. Still others rely on camouflage, meaning they are overlooked even when they are out in the open. Furthermore, many aquatic species spend much of their lives hidden in the mud and weeds in our ponds.Taking all of these factors into account, it becomes apparent that we are only likely to see a few of the species in our gardens at any one time of the 24 hour day or on any one day of the year. The total species count is therefore likely to be far higher than we realize. They only practicable way to find out how many species visit our gardens is to record them over a number of years and to regularly spend some time actively searching and observing.

We can also make additions to our gardens to encourage more species in, by providing food sources and places to breed, so that visiting individuals are more inclined to stay, rather than move on. One problem with modern gardens is that large trees are often scarce or absent, and those that do exist are seldom allowed to develop cavities and rotten limbs. This means that arboreal species have very few places to set up natural homes in suburban and urban environments. This is where it becomes important to introduce nesting boxes, roosting boxes, decaying logs, and so on, so that these species are supplied artificially with what they need.

In conclusion, the message to the reader is that we need to become less obsessive about keeping our gardens tidy and presentable. Moreover, there are ways of making gardens look presentable without making them sterile and barren to wildlife. If it matters to you, then keep the visible parts of your garden well-tended in the eyes of your neighbours but allow the hidden parts to become havens for wild animals and plants by simply leaving them to nature. It's okay to cut things back once in a while but leave it to the time of year when most species have naturally become dormant. That way, each year will see a repeat of the last, so that the flora and fauna become established without overrunning your garden.

Secondly, open your eyes and ears, so that you notice that the weeds are different plants and that the bugs are different invertebrates, and that the birds have different plumage and song. The more effort you put into noticing wildlife, the more information you will receive in return, as that is your reward; to learn and be knowledgeable about a subject that is not focussed on humanity. The reason why this is important is that it puts life into perspective, as the same wild species have been here since long before humans arrived, and throughout our history the passing generations will have been familiar those same species.

Our culture, our society, our technology, our appearance and our lifestyle have continually changed, yet there has been little change in the wilderness. It continues to ignore our presence and to reclaim its resources from us, as and when the opportunity arises. It makes one realise that the curious human ambition to tame and erase the wild is nonsense and that we are far better off working with nature for our mutual benefit.

MAMMALS

There are many species of mammal recorded in Britain, but relatively few are likely to be seen in a typical British garden. Of course, the definition of 'typical' will vary around the nation, but here we discuss those mammals that are most common in British gardens.

FOXES

The only wild Canid commonly found in British gardens is the **red fox** (*Vulpes vulpes*), often called the urban fox, because it has adapted so well to living in city gardens as well as those in the countryside. The reason for its success is that the fox is both hunter and scavenger, so it is able to make the most of a wide variety of opportunities to feed in our gardens. It is also fairly petite and able to dig tunnels and passageways, so that it can escape and hide away from dangers that may arise from people and from dogs. By keeping out of harm's way and

The red fox has become a more familiar sight in town gardens than rural gardens, because it relies more heavily on scraps and hand-outs for its food. *Don Sutherland*

generally coming out at night, the fox has free rein to exploit our gardens, almost as if they are natural habitat. Of course, people often encourage foxes in urban areas too, by feeding them, as they seldom prove a nuisance because there are few domestic chickens and ducks to safeguard.

As a general rule, foxes will hunt and kill any animal that is smaller than they are. So, they will not hesitate to feast on the domestic rabbits and guinea pigs that are often kept in gardens. For that reason, it is always wise to keep them well protected after dark. Cats and small dogs are not at risk though, as foxes will not take on other predatory animals that are likely to cause them injury.

Foxes often get a bad press as they will kill every last chicken in a coop if they manage to get inside. This is because their instinct tells them to make the most of an abundant resource, so they will return and bury their surplus quarry, to be eaten at a later date. This makes it clear that foxes will happily settle for flesh that has begun to decompose if necessary. It is an adaptation to scavenging, so that the remains of carcasses left by other predators, such as wolves, bears and large cats, can be consumed. They evidently have very high tolerance to the bacteria that would make humans quite ill, and this why they are equally at home scavenging from bins and from the detritus people drop in the street. They are also able to digest a catholic diet, which includes many waste foods in addition to meat. Although they are carnivores, they are really quite omnivorous in their eating habits. They will even eat fallen fruit from garden trees if it is all they can find.

In the wild, foxes make their dens in old badger setts and below old tree stumps, but in the urban setting they use the voids beneath houses, garages and sheds. As they are able to dig, then they will excavate their way in and then shape the den as they see fit. As long as it is dark, dry, warm, quiet and safe, then they will set up home near any reliable food source. They are naturally territorial, so foxes will fight for the best locations and are often heard squabbling over boundaries. Their population density depends on resource availability, both in terms of food and places to nest. Ironically, population densities can be far higher in urban areas than rural areas, for this reason. They mark their territories with urine to warn other foxes to stay away.

Foxes are semi-social in lifestyle, which means that they live in family groups, often comprising the grown young of the previous year as well as the new litter of kits. This means that more food can be brought back to the den and the kits have a better chance of survival to adulthood. The dominant female, or vixen, usually gives birth to 4-6 young. The dog fox and the other family members feed and protect the dominant female and her kits.

The badger is more usually seen in gardens at the transition between urban and rural areas, or large parks, where there is room for digging a sett. *Helen Haden*

BADGERS

Quite a few gardens have **badgers** (*Meles meles*) visit them at night. Badgers seldom dig their setts in gardens, as they require large areas to excavate them, but they do roam their territories in search of food. Gardens often fall within their territories, so they regularly patrol them under cover of darkness. Badgers are creatures of habit and they establish pathways, so that they can find their way back to their setts in the morning, as they have poor eyesight. As a result, they don't take kindly to having their traditional pathways obstructed and will dig their way under new fences in order to keep to their routine.

Badgers are members of the weasel family, otherwise known as Mustelids.

Like foxes, they have a varied omnivorous diet, but they are not quite so adaptable in urban environments, not least because they are more cumbersome and stocky in build and therefore less able to negotiate their way around. They are unable to leap obstacles for example, or to walk along walls. Badgers are not as strategic as foxes, as they didn't evolve as opportunistic feeders. Nor can they exploit the same kind of nesting places. While foxes are animals of the surface that prefer to hide by day, badgers are animals of the underground that emerge by night. Badgers occasionally tolerate having foxes nesting in disused parts of their setts.

Much of a badger's diet is found in the soil and rotten wood, such as earthworms, insects larvae and beetles. Although they will eat human food scraps, they generally prefer to find their own food in gardens. They will eat carrion, birds' eggs and young, slugs and snails, fruits, nuts and fungi, small mammals, reptiles and amphibians. Their activities are sometimes in evidence, where they have dug holes to extract morsels of food.

Badgers are seldom afraid of dogs, as they are equipped with powerful claws and jaws, which can inflict serious injury. They are known to eat hedgehogs, as they can roll them open and then bite at the hedgehogs where they are most vulnerable. The spiny pelt of the hedgehog is left as macabre evidence of its unfortunate fate.

STOATS AND WEASELS

The **stoat** (*Mustela ermine*) and the **weasel** (*Mustela nivalis*) are closely related, as their scientific names indicate. Although they are in the same family as the badger, they are far smaller and are adapted to a very different way of life. Both species often visit gardens, but they are very secretive and seldom seen. The stoat is somewhat larger than the weasel, and this is the reason why they are both equally common, as they don't directly compete with one another for food resources, specializing in hunting different animals.

Both the stoat and the weasel have elongated bodies, small limbs and relatively large heads. This is because they are designed to hunt burrowing mammals, so they know that if their head fits in a hole then their body can follow without getting jammed. As they are different sizes, the stoat is designed to catch rats and rabbits, whilst the weasel is designed to catch mice and voles. Both species will also raid bird nests, but again they tend to go for birds appropriate to their size. The stoat wants larger meals, and the weasel will not tackle birds big enough to fight back. As stoats and weasels are built for burrowing, they will often use the burrows and nesting

In Britain the stoat remains brownish in colour during the winter, but in some parts of Europe it turns white for camouflage in snow and is known as the ermine. *Derek Parker*

chambers of their respective prey species for their own nests. One might say that they eat them out of house and home. In gardens with plentiful supplies of prey, stoats and weasels quite often establish territories and move in, although they don't tolerate one another during the breeding season, simply because all food resources become more valuable when rearing young. Indeed, a stoat will happily hunt weasels and their young when it has its own mouths to feed.

Other species: otter, polecat, mink, pine marten.

A weasel can enter the tunnels of any small rodents as long as its head will fit, as its body is designed to neatly follow. *Ash B*

Hedgehogs are well designed for surviving in modern gardens as their spines are very good defence against any curious dogs and cats. *Peter Trimmin*

HEDGEHOGS.

The **hedgehog** (*Erinaceus europaeus*) is very familiar as a garden animal, although it is not seen particularly often, as it is nocturnal. Unfortunately, hedgehogs are more often seen as victims of road traffic. This is because their instinct is to freeze when faced with danger, so they stay put when caught in the headlights of cars and lorries. This instinct works in the wild, as they rely on their spines as an effective defence from predators, by rolling into a ball.

People quite often feed hedgehogs in their gardens, so they get used to the routine of an easy meal and become quite tame. There is a curious tradition of feeding them milk, which seems to relate to an urban myth that hedgehogs suckle from cows' udders at night. In reality, hedgehogs feed almost entirely on invertebrates, such as molluscs, worms, spiders, insects, millipedes, centipedes and woodlice. They will also eat carrion, ground-nesting birds' eggs, fruits, nuts and berries. A more appropriate food hand out would be dog or cat food. Hedgehogs cannot climb, nor can they dig, so they find their food by rummaging through leaf litter, humus and loose soil with their snouts in a similar way to pigs, which is where their name comes from. They were originally known by the name urchin, which survives with the sea urchin, a similarly spiny creature. Hedgehogs make their homes at ground level, in voids within thicket and undergrowth, or under fallen branches, which they line with dried leaves and grass. As many gardens are too tidy, the only suitable places are within compost heaps and bonfires, it is wise to check for hedgehogs before turning compost and lighting fires. Gardeners consider hedgehogs to be very useful allies in their gardens, as they hunt the slugs, snails and caterpillars that consume their cultivated flowers and vegetables. Their presence indicates good garden health, as they wouldn't visit or inhabit a garden if they had insufficient foraging opportunities. They like to roam from garden to garden, so it is good to leave places where they can pass under fences or gates on their nightly travels.

MOLES

The **mole** (*Talpa europaea*) often gets a bad press due to its habit of leaving molehills on garden lawns. In the wild, moles inhabit natural lawns, where grassland has been cropped short by herbivores, such as rabbits and deer, so our artificial lawns are very attractive to them. They prefer a short sward because it is much easier for them to excavate soil from their tunnels, as it simply falls away to form neat mounds. They prefer soft moist soil, which is easy to dig, and will avoid both waterlogged and dry soil. Moles dig their networks of tunnels to provide food, as well as somewhere to live. The tunnels function as traps for worms and other invertebrates that fall in through the soil walls. They are able to detect and grab worms at lightning speed, so that the worms don't have enough time to retract themselves into their own tunnels. As moles need to eat about half their body weight in worms each day, they require extensive lengths of tunnel, so this is why they can leave so many molehills in a relatively small area of lawn. In times of surplus, moles sometimes store worms in underground larders. Moles are very well adapted to their subterranean lifestyle. They have spade-like forepaws and silky fur to prevent the soil from sticking to their pelt. They have also virtually lost their sight, as it isn't required in the darkness of their tunnels. Instead, they have a keen sense of smell and the ability to detect vibrations rather than hearing sounds. Their skeletons are also quite rigid, so that they can push their forelimbs into the soil by clamping the tunnel behind with their hind limbs. They dig new lengths of tunnel by repeatedly shifting loads of soil along existing tunnel until they reach an exit point, where it is ejected to form a molehill. As most lawns are the centerpiece of a garden and tend to be used for human activity, then it is understandable that many people find them a nuisance. Incidentally, a good way to rid a lawn of moles is simply to flood the lawn at night. The moles will soon decide to leave under cover of darkness and move elsewhere. They naturally migrate to find new hunting grounds at night, so a little encouragement will do them no harm. Moles are seldom

Ever since the invention of the lawn, gardeners have had to contend with molehills because short-cropped grass is the perfect habitat for moles. *Wildlife Wanderer*

seen in the flesh. In fact, they are usually dead or injured when they are seen, because they have been caught above ground by domestic cats. They are not eaten, because they taste unpleasant, as do shrews, to which they are related.

SHREWS

There are two shrew species common to many British gardens. They are the **common shrew** (*Sorex araneus*) and the **pygmy shrew** (*Sorex minutus*). Just like the stoat and the weasel, the two shrews are different sizes, so that they exploit slightly different food sources. Their diet is all manner of small invertebrates, which they find by hunting through undergrowth and under roots and stones. Their differing size means that they can find and deal with different invertebrates.

Common shrews have high metabolism because their food contains few carbohydrates and they have very high surface-area-to-volume-ratio. *Kentish Plumber*

As pygmy shrews need to hunt all year they have evolved to become distasteful to predators so that more of them survive the winter. *Andrew*

Shrews are famous for having very high metabolism. Being so small, they have a very high surface to volume ratio, which means that they lose heat energy quickly. They deal with this problem by eating a great deal every day; roughly their own body weight, in fact. This high turnover of energy means that shrews produce high levels of free radicals, which in turn, means that they have very short life spans of no more than two years. The knock-on effect is that shrews have to reproduce rapidly. They can produce up to four litters of four young a year, as each brood takes about seventy days. As a pair of shrews only needs to be replaced by two more shrews, this reveals that shrews have a very high mortality rate. Even though shrews are not pleasant to taste, they are eaten by a number of garden predators, including owls, grass snakes, herons and kestrels. Shrews are well known for being very aggressive for their size, which helps them fend off other potential predators. They will not hesitate to bite a finger as thanks when rescued from the cat. The common shrew is about 110mm long, nose to tail, while the pygmy shrew is only 85mm.

Other species: water shrew.

RABBITS

The **wild rabbit** (*Oryctolagus cuniculus*) can be quite common in gardens, although it requires fairly large areas of grassland to dig its warrens, so it often only visits gardens that happen to be nearby. Rabbits eat a wide range of wild plants, but they often prefer garden plants because they are fleshy and succulent; especially the leaves of vegetables, such as brassicas, beets and lettuces. Like all animals, an easy meal to a rabbit is one that requires less time, risk and effort to fill the stomach.

Rabbits have evolved to digest their food twice in order to maximize the nutritional value. They do this by consuming their pellets at night, as they egress from the anus, so that they run through the digestive system for a second time. The droppings seen on our lawns are typically dry and fibrous, because they are the indigestible parts of the plant matter.

Of course, rabbits are known for 'breeding like rabbits'. Being a prey animal, for foxes, buzzards and stoats, they have evolved to reproduce rapidly in order to address any losses to their numbers. Many are also shot for the pot by humans, or simply exterminated as pests. In the 1970s, rabbits were struck by a viral illness called myxomatosis. It is an unpleasant disease that causes tumours and secondary bacterial infections, turning rabbits blind and eventually killing them. However, their prolific ability to reproduce meant that rabbits were able to evolve resistance to the affliction. Individuals that happened to be immune passed on their genes, so that the rabbit populations

The wild rabbit is often attracted to gardens and allotments because it likes to eat the same tender stems and leaves of vegetables that we like to eat.

recovered. This is what is meant by natural selection, as those animals able to survive were effectively selected by nature to continue the rabbit line and change the genepool. The same process happens all the time, with all species, so that slight adjustments with each generation enable them to adapt to changes in their environment. We only notice though, when significant changes are made. This is why the individuals that make up any population are slightly different in size, shape, markings, behaviour and so on, as the variation allows evolution to occur.

Other species: hare.

SQUIRRELS

There are two types of squirrel seen in British gardens; the **red squirrel** (*Sciurus vulgaris*) and the grey squirrel (Sciurus carolinensis). Somewhat ironically, the scientific name of the red squirrel means 'common squirrel' even though it is now far less common than the grey squirrel. This is because the grey squirrel was introduced from America and has replaced the native species in many places.

However, it turns out that grey squirrels are not well adapted to living in pine forests, as only red squirrels can extract the seeds from pinecones. As a result, we now have distinct populations of grey and red squirrels in

In coniferous woodland the red squirrel does very well because it is able to exploit the pinecones for their pine nuts as food. *Peter Trimming*

different areas. This means that some people only see red squirrels in their gardens, while other people only see grey squirrels. The names 'red' and 'grey' can be misleading as both species vary quite a bit in colour, with some overlap. They are different sizes, but as they are never seen together then a comparison cannot be made either. So, if in doubt, a reliable way to identify them is by looking at the ears. Red squirrels have tufts on their ears, while grey squirrels never do. Both species of squirrel will visit feeders to take nuts and seeds, although this is often a nuisance when the food is intended for birds. Squirrels can also be pests in gardens by feeding on buds, fruits and nuts on trees and shrubs. So, it can be wise to deliberately feed them, so that they are diverted away from valued flowers and crops. It is far better to work with nature than fight a losing battle.

In deciduous woodland the grey squirrel out competes the red squirrel because it is a larger and more aggressive species.

In reality, squirrels are tree-living rats, but there is no denying that they have a more appealing appearance to the human eye due to their bushy tails and their more rounded faces. The way they use their forelimbs to manipulate their food also lends them an anthropomorphic or human-like quality, so that squirrels are often highly regarded as garden visitors: i.e. they are 'cute' to look at.

DORMICE

Of the two types of British dormouse, the **edible dormouse** (*Glis glis*) is the more likely to be found in people's gardens. It is adapted to arboreal life much like squirrels and is quite common in one area of Britain, but absent elsewhere. Unlike squirrels, edible dormice are crepuscular and nocturnal. They are often heard crawling around in loft spaces, where they make their nests, although they will also use large cavities in old trees or suitably sized nest boxes.

The edible dormouse is so called because it was once reared and eaten by the Romans who used large earthenware storage jars as cages and fattened

Dormouse: The edible dormouse is quite common in certain areas, where its presence is often noticed by the sound of movement in the eaves of houses where it nests. *Francesca*

Hazel Dormouse: The hazel dormouse is seldom seen in the flesh, but its presence is often betrayed by the shells of hazelnuts found with perfectly gnawed round holes. *Kentish Plumber*

the dormice ready for the dinner table. Squirrels are eaten in parts of the USA as they also make good eating. The Romans didn't introduce the edible dormouse to Britain. They escaped from a zoological collection over a century ago and have established a population across the lower Midlands. It is possible that a few rural gardens have the **hazel dormouse** (*Muscardinus avellanarius*) in residence, as it is more widespread in Britain. It requires hazel coppice, rather than hazel woodland, as its habitat, which is why the species has become scarce, as basket weaving and besom making are no longer practiced. The two species are not closely related, but they belong to the same family and have characteristic fury tails. The hazel dormouse is far smaller and mouse-like. Both species hibernate overwinter, because they cannot find sufficient food, as they are not as adaptable as squirrels due to their nocturnal habits. They are nocturnal because they cannot run and leap through forest canopy to escape predators as squirrels do. Nor can they run very fast on the ground.

BATS

Although bats are usually only seen fleetingly on warm summer evenings, as they patrol our gardens for insects, they are surprisingly abundant. In fact, there are seventeen species resident across Britain, making them the most successful of our mammal families. There are so many species because they have adapted to fill different econiches in the night skies and therefore avoid direct competition for food.

They vary in size, so that they specialize in catching different sized prey. They fly at different heights, so that they encounter different prey. Some

The pipistrelle bat is one of our commonest bats, and is able to roost in small spaces, such as under facia boards, behind shutters and in wall voids. *Mark Rosher*

The noctule bat feeds on large flying insects, so it is more likely to be see in larger gardens that include mature trees, or gardens close to woodland. *Jan Svetlik*

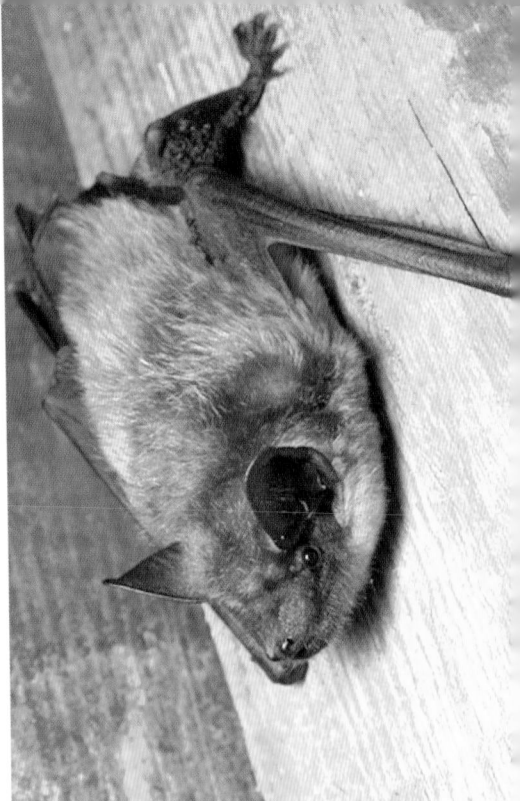

The brown long-eared bat is a species that needs open voids in order to land and roost by hanging freely, such as loft spaces. *Sarah Louise Winch*

The serotine bat, sometimes known as the evening bat, is a relatively large species with a wingspan of about 15inch (370mm). *Markus Knolf*

hunt in open spaces, whilst other hunt in woodland. Some specialize in hunting low over bodies of water and will take insects from the surface. Some specialize in taking spiders and caterpillars from foliage, while others only take flying insects. Some have relatively good eyesight, so they can hunt early in the evening and catch day-flying insects such as butterflies, dragonflies, damselflies and beetles. Others rely entirely on echolocation to hunt in complete darkness. Although most people think bats eat moths, they actually feed on a wide range of other invertebrates. Echolocation is a way of locating prey and obstacles by detecting echoes made by sound waves. Bats emit high frequency calls, which strike and bounce off objects back to their ears. They use these echoes to 'see' in the dark, as their brains interpret the information in much the same way that information is interpreted by our eyes. As sound waves travel at just under 770 mph, then bats are generally pretty good at striking prey and avoiding collisions. The common teasel plant (*Dipsacus fullonum*) is known to catch bats. When certain bat species attempt to catch insects roosting on the plants, their fuzzy seed heads latch onto the fur of the bats, much like Velcro. The bats then die and fertilize the soil beneath the plants for the following year's seeds. It used to be thought that the fuzzy seed heads evolved to spread the seeds by latching onto the fur of deer and so forth, but there is no evidence for this as the plants remain intact long after the seeds have fallen. Bats have a very slow rate of reproduction. Females cannot afford to carry too much weight whilst pregnant, as they need to be able to hunt on the wing. This means that they produce just one offspring per year. However, bats live incredibly long lives for their size – up to thirty years in fact. Therefore, they are still able to reproduce sufficient offspring to keep the population stable. When compared with shrews, which have a similar diet and size, bats achieve this feat of longevity by hibernating and by becoming dormant during the day. It means that they burn far less fuel to stay alive by lowering their metabolism. In turn, this produces far lower levels of free radicals, so they can live far longer than shrews. Bats use a number of different roosts. There are breeding roosts, where the females rear their offspring. There are days roosts, where males hideout during daylight hours. There are hibernation roosts where males and females secrete themselves during the winter months. The physical nature of their roosts also depends on the species of bat. Some species are able to land and then crawl into tight spaces, whilst others need to able to fly up to their perches. The reason why they roost upside down is partly to save energy, as they simply hang from their claws. It also enables them to use places that cannot be reached by predators, with the added advantage that they can simply take flight by dropping downwards. Typical bat species seen in our gardens are the **common pipistrelle** (*Pipistrellus pipistrellus*), the **common noctule** (*Nyctalus noctula*), the **brown long-eared** (*Plecotus auritus*) and the **serotine** (*Eptesicus serotinus*). These species are all found in rural, suburban and urban environments where they make the most of our garden habitats and our buildings.

RATS, MICE AND VOLES

The mammals always viewed as varmints and villains in our gardens are rats and mice. The most common species around human habitations are the **brown rat** (*Rattus norvegicus*) and the **house mouse** (*Mus musculus*). Both species have very cosmopolitan omnivorous diets, which makes them very well suited to surviving on the waste foods we leave in our bins, on compost heaps and on bird tables. Of course, they often raid our larders and cupboards too. In fact, they can rely solely on our groceries and scraps, never bothering to find food elsewhere.

Being considerably smaller, mice are able to find their way through surprisingly small gaps and holes, making them quite difficult to eradicate from our homes. Rats are far larger, so tend to remain outside and make their homes under sheds

The brown rat does very well living alongside humans, because it will eat virtually any food scraps that we put in our bins, on our compost heaps and on our lawns. *Pete Beard*

and in outhouses. Both species are multivoltine, meaning they have several broods each year and can therefore increase their populations quite rapidly when the pickings are good. This is helped by living in the proximity of humans, as they are often able to keep their litters suitably warm during the winter months. In the garden, rats and mice can wreak havoc with domestic crops, in fruit and vegetable plots and in greenhouses. This is especially so when there are few natural predators

The house mouse is extremely good at living in our homes, because it is so small and can find food and shelter often without us noticing. *Stefan Jurgensen*

f Tscher

Hanna Knutsson

The field vole *(left)* has smaller ears and a shorter tail than the bank vole *(right)*, so that it can more easily escape predators by diving into tunnels when it is being hunted out in the open.

about, which is a good reason for restoring the ecological balance in our gardens. Owls, hawks, falcons, stoats and weasels are all effective at controlling rat and mouse numbers.

In suburban and rural gardens, it is likely that other small rodents frequent

The wood mouse *(left)* is adapted for woodland floor, while the yellow-necked mouse *(right)* is adapted for climbing, so it has longer limbs and tail.

anna Knutsson

Stinelk

gardens, such as the **wood mouse** (*Apodemus sylvaticus*), the **yellow-necked mouse** (*Apodemus flavicollis*), the **bank vole** (*Clethrionomys glareolus*) and the **field vole** (*Microtus agrestis*). None of these species should be considered a pest, as they are part of British natural history, whilst the brown rat and house mouse have both been introduced by the historical activities of humanity.

Both of the wild mouse species are adapted for climbing amongst undergrowth, as well as running on the ground. Their limbs are therefore longer than the house mouse and they also have chestnut brown pelts, rather than grey. The vole species are adapted for running along passageways that they make in the undersward of long grass, so they have short limbs and tails. All four species feed primarily on shoots, wild seeds, nuts and fruits, with the occasional insect for protein. They are usually only seen by people when domestic cats bring them into the house as trophies, either dead or still alive. In the wild, they are staple foods for carnivorous mammals, birds of prey and other large birds, including those in the crow family and herons. Snakes also eat small rodents and their young, when they find a nest.

Other species: black rat, water vole, harvest mouse.

DEER

By far the most ubiquitous of the British deer species is the **roe deer** (*Capreolus capreolus*). It is native to our lands and is adapted to life in natural woodland with scattered patches of grassland. It therefore views gardens as an extension of its natural habitat and is familiar to many who live in rural and suburban areas.

During the congenial months, roe deer browse and forage on the buds, flowers and foliage of many and various types of plant. This is partly to ensure a varied diet but is also means that they avoid poisoning themselves too badly should they happen to eat something toxic. Roe deer therefore have a reputation for eating cultivars in people's gardens, as they are naturally drawn to eating plants they haven't seen before, especially if they are soft and palatable. Some people install electric fences or close off their gardens with high fencing if the problem becomes intolerable, even though it might be considered excessive. It can be argued that it is far nicer to see deer on one's lawn, even if they do nibble the odd plant. Roe deer are very sleek and nimble animals, able to run through dense thicket and leap surprisingly high obstacles. This is testament to their evolution, in order to escape erstwhile predators, such as wolves, bears and lynx. With the modern absence of predators, they sometimes need to be culled by marksmen, to keep their numbers at a healthy level. The roe deer has its name, because roe derives from Old English meaning mottled or spotted, alluding to the camouflaged coat of the deer fawn.

The roe deer is an elegant animal, designed for running and jumping through woodland, making garden fences very easy to leap. *Fra298*

The fallow deer is the quintessential deer often seen on Christmas cards, as its spotted pelt and large antlers make it pleasing to the eye. *Tony Hisgett*

Stockier and less nimble, is the **fallow deer** (*Dama dama*), which is locally common in Britain, having been introduced by the Romans, but less widespread than the roe deer. It has its name because it was often seen grazing fallow fields during the Mediaeval period. They are more comfortable on open ground or in mature woodland, not least because they sport large antlers that would otherwise impede their movements. Fallow deer also roam in larger herds for protection and can cause considerable crop damage. They will occasionally enter gardens if they happen to border the fields and woodland they naturally frequent.

The **barking deer** (*Muntiacus reevesi*), which was introduced in the twentieth century, has become naturalized in some parts of Britain. Unlike the roe deer and fallow deer, the barking deer is quite small and pig-like, preferring to live in thick undergrowth or thicket, and often becoming more active at night. It is seldom seen, but its barking is often heard in the darkness, which sounds rather harsh and haunting, as if it were some mythical creature in pain. In fact, it is a mating and contact call, so that the deer can find one another. The barking deer visits many gardens unnoticed due to its secretive and nocturnal habits, and its browsing is often blamed on other animals.

Other species: red deer, water deer, sika deer.

The barking deer is adapted to life in thick undergrowth, so it is often seen skulking beneath garden hedges and shrubs, rather than grazing in the open. *Whistling Joe*

BIRDS

SPARROWHAWK

The **sparrowhawk** (*Accipiter nisus*) is the quintessential garden bird of prey, because it is perfectly adapted for hunting by ambushing small birds in woodland clearings. It has rounded wings that enable it to stealthily fly between the branches of trees and then strike its prey unawares.

The female sparrowhawk is larger than the male, enabling both genders

As its name suggests, the sparrowhawk will prey on sparrows and many other small to medium sized species of garden bird.

John Boyle

to focus on catching different sized prey. The male will go for birds as big as thrushes, while the female go for birds as big as jackdaws and woodpeckers. This increases the range of potential prey, so that offspring are more likely to be fed and survive into adulthood. The sparrowhawk is so feared by other birds that the cuckoo has evolved to mimic its appearance. This enables the female cuckoo to lay its eggs in the nests of other birds, because they instinctively go into hiding when they mistakenly sense danger. Sparrowhawks also soar high in the sky in order to reconnoitre the landscape for places that may provide good hunting. When they spot a flock of feeding or roosting birds they then descend some distance away and approach from the side, undercover, to try their luck. Gardens provide bountiful hunting in this regard as passerines, and other garden birds, are often distracted by bird tables and bird feeders. Gardens also provide the right kind of habitat, as they have open spaces surrounded by bushes and hedges. Like many raptors, sparrowhawks nest in large trees, so most gardens don't offer suitable locations. They therefore use gardens as their hunting grounds and nest in trees some distance away. When teaching their young to fly, the adults will fly ahead with food, as if a light aircraft pulling a glider on a rope. The fledgling calls repeatedly with a characteristic mewing sound.

TAWNY OWL.

Just as the sparrowhawk is the perfect garden predator during the day, the **tawny owl** (*Strix aluco*) is the perfect garden predator during the night. This is why both are widespread and successful birds of prey. The tawny owl hunts ground-living rodents by sitting on perches and swooping down when it hears or sees movement. It also hunts roosting birds, as large as crows. Small prey are swallowed whole, while larger prey are carried back to the nest and butchered.

The wings of the tawny owl are large and rounded, partly so that it can fly between tree branches, but also to enable vertical takeoffs from undergrowth when the bird has made a kill. They are also equipped with special feathers, which reduce the sound they make during flight. Tawny owls have stereoscopic vision, so that they are able to accurately judge distance. They also have asymmetrically placed ears, so that they can locate sounds accurately. The famous two-part call of the tawny owl – twit:twoo – is traditionally believed to be a combination of the female and male calls. This isn't strictly true, as both halves of the call can often be heard repeatedly in isolation, and both genders can make both. So, it may be true sometimes, but not always. Tawny owls typically require cavities in large trees for nesting, so they seldom

The tawny owl is a successful garden bird because it will prey on a variety of animals, including small mammals, birds, reptiles, amphibians and insects. *Colin Haycock*

actually nest within gardens. They will also nest in the boughs of large trees, often using the old nest of similarly sized birds. They will also use nest boxes, but they need to be suitably large and positioned in suitable places. As the birds roost during the day, they have evolved camouflaged plumage, making them virtually invisible against the bark of trees.

Other species: Little Owl, Barn Owl, Buzzard, Kestrel.

CROWS

The **carrion crow** (*Corvus corone*) is a common bird in rural, suburban and urban gardens. It is a versatile species with an omnivorous diet, which includes scraps of food. It also exploits road kill and will sometimes actively hunt pigeons. It therefore manages to find plenty to eat in and around gardens. Being a large bird, it also intimidates smaller birds, so that it gets first pickings. Crows nest in the canopy of medium to large trees, which are often found in gardens and in parks, so they tend to have everything they need by living alongside humans. In northern regions, the carrion crow is replaced by the **hooded crow** (*Corvus cornix*), which is identical aside from its grey plumage. In fact, the two birds are so closely related that they sometimes hybridize.

The **carrion crow** (*left*) and the **hooded crow** (*right*) are closely related and will interbreed when their ranges meet in the north.

Like the rook, the jackdaw lives communally, although it nests on roofs and chimneys rather than in trees.

The **jackdaw** (*Corvus monedula*) is even more adaptable than the carrion crow, as it is smaller and able to exploit chimneys tops and ledges for nesting. Jackdaws will actually nest inside chimneys too, by dropping sticks inside until they become wedged and enable the birds to build a platform.

The jackdaw is a social species and lives in colonies within towns, which can span many gardens. Being social has the benefit of providing strength in numbers, enabling the jackdaw to fend off predators and to take over feeding opportunities from other birds. The jackdaw is an intelligent and inquisitive bird. Occasionally juvenile birds are naturally tame and will befriend people when fed. They make good pets and have a curious attraction to colourful and shiny objects, which they will snatch as trophies. It seems that their association with people has lasted so long that it has largely removed their innate fear genetically. This is sometimes seen in other urbanized species too, because natural selection no longer favours fearful behaviour.

The **magpie** (*Pica pica*) is a semi-social species. It nests in isolation but tends to roam in small groups: hence the rhyme 'one for sorrow, two for joy, three for a girl, four for a boy, five for silver, six for gold, seven for a story never to be told'. The nest of the magpie takes the form of a ball of sticks, with a chamber inside. This protects the eggs and young from marauding predators, including crows and jackdaws. It also enables the magpie to nest in small trees that would not support a conventional nest, because the nest knits a number of thin branches together. As a result, magpies are common garden birds in many areas. Like most other crow family species, magpies have catholic tastes and reasonable intelligence, so they are able to exploit human environments.

Magpies are usually seen in ones or twos during the summer but will roam in larger family groups during the winter.

The jay looks decidedly exotic for a crow, especially with the flashes of blue on its wings.

The **jay** (*Garrulus glandarius*) is the least crow-like of its family in appearance. In fact, it looks quite exotic with its mix of brown, white, black and blue plumage. Jays tend to be more secretive than other crows, but they are fairly common in large rural and suburban gardens. The jay feeds on a variety of items, ranging from nuts and fruits to invertebrates, eggs and the young of other birds. The jay has a particular association with oak trees, because it likes to hoard acorns in the autumn months, as a cache of food for winter. So, where there are oak trees, there tend to be jays. The jay also has an association with Formica ant nests. It 'bathes' in ants by spreading its wings over a nest, so that the ants defend their nest by spraying formic acid. The acid penetrates the jay's plumage and rids the jay of parasitic bird lice.

The **rook** (*Corvus frugilegus*) is rather similar in appearance to its close relative the crow. It differs primarily in having a naked face, which is an adaptation to probing the ground in search of earthworms and various insect larvae, so that it doesn't become clogged with mud and detritus. The rook will also eat a variety of other foodstuffs, including tidbits dropped by people. It has therefore adjusted to living alongside humans in suburban areas. Rooks

The rook is sometimes seen on garden lawns, where it hunts for worms and any other invertebrates it may find.

nest communally in rookeries, which are clusters of nests seen in the canopies of stands of mature trees. They tend to nest in parks, where suitable trees are found, and forage in nearby gardens.

Other species: raven.

WOODPECKERS, NUTHATCH AND TREECREEPER

The **green woodpecker** (*Picus viridis*) is well known for its call, which is reminiscent of a histrionic human laugh. This is why the bird is sometimes known as the yaffle. It is a large and handsome bird, with plumage in complementary colours of green and red. In addition to eating insect larvae found in soft rotten wood, the green woodpecker is rather fond of eating ants. It is therefore often seen on garden lawns, where it finds and opens ant nests to extract the insects and their larvae and the pupae. It has a long sticky tongue for collecting the insects. In effect, it is a winged anteater.

Being a fairly large bird, the green woodpecker requires cavities in large

The green woodpecker is equally at home on the ground as it is in trees, where it feeds on ants. *Phil McIver*

trees for nesting. It has a relatively weak beak, so it often uses the old nest holes of the greater spotted woodpecker. Like other woodpeckers, the green woodpecker has an undulating flight, which means that it follows a wave-like path, because it flaps its wings intermittently.

The **greater spotted woodpecker** (*Dendrocopos major*) is an equally striking species, this time black and white against the red. It is better adapted to chiseling wood than the green woodpecker and can excavate living wood to make its nest holes if rotten trees are not available. It also has a barbed tongue, for hooking out wood boring larvae of beetles and moths. Its skull is adapted to absorbing the shock waves of pecking wood, so that its brain is not traumatized. Greater spotted woodpeckers are more likely to visit bird feeders than green woodpeckers, as they are particularly attracted to fat. Both species will use nest boxes as alternatives to trees. They like nest boxes filled with a soft material mimicking decayed wood, such as expanded polystyrene or polyurethane foam, so that they can excavate a cavity to their exact specifications.

The **lesser spotted woodpecker** (*Dryobates minor*) has similar plumage to the greater spotted woodpecker, but is far smaller, being adapted to exploit tree branches

The lesser-spotted woodpecker is often overlooked in gardens, because it is quite small and secretive. *SateAlAbbasi.*

The greater-spotted woodpecker is fairly common in gardens and will often come to bird feeders in winter. *Sue Cro*

The nuthatch is a rather neat looking bird that will often visit bird feeders to take nuts. *PhotoApe*

The treecreeper hunts by spiralling up trunks trees and is well camouflaged against the bark. *Jan Svetlik*

rather than tree trunks. It is far less commonly seen in gardens, and often overlooked anyway due to its diminutive size. It has become quite uncommon in recent years because rotten old trees are rapidly cleared away from farms, parks and gardens due to excessive health and safety concerns, leaving the birds with fewer resources for feeding and nesting in agricultural and suburban areas. If instead, the trees had their branches truncated and were otherwise left standing then all woodpeckers would benefit, not to mention wood boring insects and other cavity nesting birds.

While the woodpeckers specialize in feeding on invertebrates beneath the surface of tree trunks and branches, the **nuthatch** (*Sitta europaea*) and the **treecreeper** (*Certhia familiaris*) specialize in finding invertebrates on and under the bark of trees. Both species have adapted to subtly different food resources, as the nuthatch works its way down a tree, whilst the treecreeper works its way up a tree. As a result, they discover invertebrates hidden in different places. The nuthatch also has the habit of lodging hazelnuts and acorns between the grooves in the bark of large trees, so that it can peck them open. They also make for a cache of accessible food in the winter.

Other species: wryneck.

PIGEONS

The terms *dove* and *pigeon* are interchangeable, even though the former tends to evoke an image of a bird more petite and delicate than the latter. The term *dove* derives from Old Norse, whilst the term *pigeon* derives from Latin.

Peter Richman

Dave Curtis

The rock dove *(above)*, **stock dove** *(right top)* and **wood pigeon** *(right)* are quite similar, so many people fail to notice the different species.

Catherine Thackstone

In fact, the **town pigeon**, **racing pigeons** and **show pigeons** (*Columba livia domestica*) are all descended from the **rock dove** (*Columba livia*). Although town pigeons are often seen in town and city gardens, they are less often seen in rural gardens, because they are replaced by wild species. This is largely because town pigeons naturally nest on building ledges that substitute for the cliffs upon which wild rock doves nest, so they prefer urban locations. Another reason why town pigeons do so well in the most urban of settings is that they do not feed their young directly with the scraps they scavenge. Instead, they produce a secretion from their crops, which is known as *crop milk*. Thus, the adults can convert their harlequin diet into suitable food for their chicks.

The **wood pigeon** (*Columba palumbus*) and the **stock dove** (*Columba oenas*) are similar in appearance to the classic town pigeon, as all three have generally grey plumage with pinkish breasts and black bars on the wings. In rural areas the wood pigeon and stock dove are more likely to be seen, as they are both tree nesters. The wood pigeon is told by the white marks on each side of

Tony Sutton

The turtle dove *(above)* and the ring-necked dove *(below)* are smaller than other species and have a base colour of beige instead of grey.

Alex RF

the neck, while the stock dove is told by its wings having less defined black bars. The wood pigeon is also larger than the stock dove, although this is only usually evident when both species are seen together.

The **ring-necked dove** (*Streptopelia capicola*) and the **turtle dove** (*Streptopelia turtur*) are occasionally seen in gardens, although they are really birds of open ground, so they prefer fields, meadows, heathland and moorland. Their plumage betrays the fact that they are adapted to foraging on bare ground for seeds, where they are camouflaged against dry soil. The ring-necked dove is resident in Britain, while the turtle dove is a summer visitor from North

Africa. Both species have declined in numbers because farming techniques have become more efficient, so that seeds are spilled in lower numbers. The birds are sometimes attracted to gardens where birdseed can be found scattered on lawns and patios. The ring-necked dove is resident because it is more adaptable in its diet than the turtle dove, so it doesn't need to migrate.

HERONS

The **grey heron** (*Ardea cinerea*) has learnt to exploit garden ponds in rural, suburban and urban areas. It nests communally in large trees usually some distance from the gardens it plunders, but it is capable of flying many miles. Its large size enables it to carry large cargoes of fish, frogs, birds and rodents

The heron is attracted to garden ponds with goldfish because they are so easy to see and catch. *Smudge 9000*

back to its young. The heron is well designed for landing and taking off in confined spaces, because its natural feedings sites are clearings between trees along the sides of river and lakes. This makes it perfectly suited to raiding garden ponds.

Of course, the fish in most garden ponds are unable to escape to deeper water, as they would in the wild, so the heron usually has no problem feasting on the entire population in a short space of time, especially when they happen to be highly visible gold fish, golden orfe or koi carp. We like these fish in our ponds because they are brightly coloured, but that is their undoing when a heron come along. People often discover their ponds to be entirely empty of fish as a result. Rather than covering ponds with unsightly mesh or netting, it is far better to put bridges across, so that the fish have somewhere to hide from herons. It is also good to have deep areas with parts of the pond encroached by shrubs, so that a heron would find it difficult to reach the fish. Alternatively, one might have a wildlife pond, where fish are absent, so that amphibians and invertebrates can thrive without being preyed upon.

Other species: little egret.

THRUSHES AND STARLING

Some of our most familiar garden birds are among the thrush family. The **blackbird** (*Turdus merula*) is common in rural, suburban and urban gardens, where it feeds on lawns and in flowerbeds in search of earthworms and other invertebrates. The bird used to be known as the ouzel, which is why there is a related mountain-living species known as the ring ouzel (*T. torquatus*). In fact, the dipper (*Cinclus cinclus*), was once called the water ouzel, due to its having a similar appearance even though it is not a thrush.

The blackbird is a successful garden bird because its natural habitat is essentially the same, comprising clearings in woodland, where it finds earthworms in the soil and beneath leaf litter. It also nests in any available recess that is safe from predators and protected from the weather, so it often finds suitable places in garden hedges and bushes. It will also use ledges in sheds and outhouses if undisturbed, as well as open-fronted bird boxes installed with appropriate privacy.

The **song thrush** (*Turdus philomelos*) is another frequent garden visitor. As its name suggests, it has a strong and melodic song, much the same as the male blackbird, except that it tends to repeat phrases. The song thrush specializes in eating snails, which it consumes by bashing against a stone anvil until their shells break away. The broken shells of various different snail species can often be found scattered around such stones.

One of the most common
garden birds, the blackbird
is usually seen in ones
or twos on lawns, or in
flowerbeds, looking for
worms. The female is
brown rather than black.

Tim Oxe

The song thrush is the only garden bird that has developed a technique for eating snails, so it has a ready supply of food throughout the year. *Derek Parker*

The mistle thrush is responsible for spreading the seeds of mistletoe, which is a parasitic plant that lives on the branches of trees.

Don Sutherlan

During the winter months, redwings *(above)* and fieldfares *(below)* roam British gardens in search of berries and fallen fruits to eat.

The **mistle thrush** *(Turdus viscivorus)* has its name due to its fondness for eating the berries of mistletoe. It also eats the berries of holly and will often establish territories where these plants are present. It prefers habitat that is more open, so tends to be seen more often in larger gardens.

The **redwing** *(Turdus iliacus)* and the **fieldfare** *(Turdus pilaris)* are both winter visitors from northern Europe. They roam gardens in search of berries and fallen fruits and can often be seen in mixed flocks. Like the other thrushes,

The starling is a lawn and meadow specialist, where it will hunt for worms in flocks. *DiddlecomeDawcock*

they also eat a wide variety of invertebrates and visit bird tables.

The name **starling** (*Sturnus vulgaris*) alludes to the fact that the bird's summer plumage looks like the night sky covered in tiny stars: thus star-ling, which is rather romantic. The starling looks similar to the blackbird, and is also often seen on lawns looking for earthworms and insect larvae. It has the habit of probing the turf with an open beak, so that it can quickly seize its prey when it feels movement. It prefers more open habitat to the blackbird and can often be seen on the greens and verges in housing estates. It is a hole-nester in the wild, so it likes to nest in cavities beneath the eaves of houses. These have become scarce in the modern era due to the use of PVC soffits, so the birds benefit from suitable bird boxes. Their numbers have fallen for this reason, but they are still common in suitable locations. Starlings are well known for their large flocks, which descend into trees and marshes to roost. The natural flight movements, as they avoid collisions, among the thousands of birds result in interesting waves and flow patterns. These natural wonders are known as murmuration exaltations.

FLYCATCHERS

The flycatchers, as their name suggests, are primarily hunters of small flying insects, although they will often eat other invertebrates too. They are in the habit of using lookout posts, from which they fly sorties whenever they see something to catch. The **robin** (*Erithacus rubecula*) can be seen doing this from the lower branch of a tree or the handle of a spade, darting off to collect an insect or a small earthworm from the ground and then returning. The **spotted flycatcher** (*Muscicapa striata*) on the other hand, does so from higher branches

Unlike the spotted flycatcher and the nightingale, the robin remains in our gardens during the winter months. *Kentish Plumber*

The spotted flycatcher has a distinctively upright sitting posture, so that it can more easily launch itself in any direction after its prey. *AndyMorffew*

and wires, and catches its prey in mid-air. Thus, the two species are adapted to exploit slightly different food sources. The spotted flycatcher is a summer visitor, as it needs to go elsewhere in the winter to catch its food, whilst the robin is more adaptable, as it will make do with berries and seeds in the winter.

If the robin is well known for its song in British gardens, then the **nightingale**

(*Luscinia megarhynchos*) is positively famous for its vocal abilities. In truth, although the nightingale is certainly able to produce a remarkable repertoire of sounds, it is far less mellifluous and pleasant to listen to than the robin. This is because the nightingale runs through a list of different sounds, as if it were trying out the quirky settings on an electronic keyboard, which therefore sounds rather disjointed and non sequitur. The robin, on the other hand, actually sings with expression and narrative flow. Nightingales have become less common in gardens over recent years due to people's anal tidiness. Nightingales nest close to the ground, so they need dense and overgrown thicket in order to protect their nests from predators. As a result, they only successfully nest in large gardens with suitably unkempt corners of undergrowth.

Other species: pied flycatcher, redstart, stonechat.

The nightingale uses its song as a signal so that other nightingales are able to find it in woodland during a brief breeding season. *RazEtCharlotte*

Billy Lindblom

Ron Knight

Ron Knight

The chiffchaff *(top left)*, **garden warbler** *(top right)*, **willow warbler** *(bottom left)* and **wood warbler** *(bottom right)* are quite tricky to tell apart in the field, but their calls and songs are quite different from one another.

WARBLERS

Similar to the flycatchers is the large family of birds known as warblers. They are also insectivorous and tend to have rather dull plumage like the nightingale and the spotted flycatcher. As a result, many species are quite difficult to tell apart visually. In our gardens we are most likely to see the **chiffchaff** (*Phylloscopus collybita*), the **willow warbler** (*Phylloscopus trochilus*), the **wood warbler** (*Phylloscopus sibilatrix*) the **garden warbler** (*Sylvia borin*), the **blackcap** (*Sylvia atricapilla*), the **whitethroat** (*Sylvia communis*) and the **lesser whitethroat** (*Sylvia curruca*).

All five species live in deciduous woodland and clearings in the wild setting, so gardens present familiar habitat to them. They tend to remain obscured by

Kentish Plumber

The blackcap is unusual among the woodland warblers in having its distinctive black crown. The female has a fulvous brown crown.

the foliage of tree and shrubs, so they are often overlooked. The first four species are known as leaf warblers, whilst the other two are known as typical warblers. The most striking of the five species is the blackcap, as the male has a distinctive black crown, whilst the female has a fulvous crown. The other species are muted browns and greens, making them well camouflaged in the canopy.

As its name suggests, the lesser white throat is slightly smaller than the whitethroat.

noFonsaGrada

HederaBaltica

The best way to tell them apart in the field is often by their song, but then it is necessary to learn their different songs, which isn't easy either. They are known as warblers because they often have warbling songs, which means that they have rapidly repeated notation or vibrato.

Other species: reed warbler, sedge warbler, grasshopper warbler.

WAGTAILS AND PIPITS

Wagtails are very much like warblers, except that they are adapted to walking and hunting on the ground, rather than in trees. They are insectivorous and often take advantage of seasonal gluts in flies, mosquitos and other flying insects on or near ponds, as well as lawns and driveways.

The most common of these birds is the **white** or **pied wagtail** (*Motacilla alba*), which is often seen in urban areas, as well as suburban and rural. This is because it likes to hunt for prey on open ground, so the most uninviting path of tarmac or concrete can be an attractive prospect. The same goes for roofs, especially flat roofs on garages and so on. The tail wagging is counterintuitive, for it actually serves to hide the bird from predators, as it mimics an inanimate object oscillating in a breeze.

The **grey wagtail** (*Motacilla cinerea*) is commonly confused with the **yellow wagtail** (*Motacilla flava*), as both have yellow bellies. However, the grey wagtail

Yellow Wagtail.

has a grey back, whilst the yellow wagtail has an olive back. These species are usually only seen in gardens with ponds or nearby bodies of water. All three wagtails have a habit of suddenly running to catch grounded insects, or else leaping into the air to snap at airborne insects.

Other species: wood pipit, meadow pipit, rock pipit, wood lark, skylark.

FINCHES, BUNTINGS AND SPARROWS

These are the seedeaters among the garden birds. They have relatively robust bills, with each suited to different types of buds, berries, fruits, seeds, nuts, pits and so on. Among the finches are some of the most colourful garden birds, including the **gold finch** (*Carduelis carduelis*), the **chaffinch** (*Fringilla coelebs*), the **brambling** (*Fringilla montifringilla*), the **bullfinch** (*Pyrrhula pyrrhula*), the **siskin** (*Spinus spinus*) and the **greenfinch** (*Chloris chloris*). During the winter months, these species can be seen roaming gardens in mixed flocks. They will readily come to bird tables and feeders, where they are a pleasure to watch. The **common redpoll**

The goldfinch is surprisingly colourful for a British bird and is often seen feeding on the seed-heads of thistles. *Kentish Plumber*

The chaffinch is a smart looking bird with neat plumage reminiscent of a military uniform from the nineteenth century. *Noel Reynolds*

The brambling is similar to the chaffinch, but its uniform is rather less clearly defined. *Richard Towell*

The bullfinch is conspicuous in flight due to its bright red breast and its white rump. *Sergey Yeliseev*

As its name suggests, the greenfinch has plumage comprising various hues and shades of green. *Jan Svetlik*

Both the common redpoll *(left)* and the lesser redpoll *(right)* can be mistaken for sparrows, except that they have red-pink foreheads.

Ron Knight

Nat Engl

The crossbill has an overlapping mandible especially adapted for removing the seeds from pinecones. *Martha De Jong-Lantik*

(*Acanthis flammea*) and **lesser redpoll** (*Acanthis cabaret*) are less conspicuous finches. They look rather like sparrows, but with reddish spots on their crowns. There are two finch species with peculiar bills adapted for removing the seeds from pine cones. They are the **crossbill** (*Loxia curvirostra*) and the **Scottish crossbill** (*Loxia scotica*). The latter is the only bird species endemic to Britain.

The siskin has a fine bill for a finch, as it is adapted for eating small and soft seeds.

Allan Hopkins

The yellowhammer is often seem singing loudly whilst perched on top of hedges.

The corn bunting is easily mistaken for a sparrow, as it has cryptic brown plumage. *Alistair Rae*

The name 'cirl' (pronounced sirl) is derived from Italian for 'chirp', due to its call. *Fra 298*

Although it nests in reed beds, the reed bunting roams through gardens during the winter in search of seeds. *Ian Preston*

Buntings are very similar to finches, but their colours are generally more tertiary greens, mustards and browns. They are also more rural in their habits. A few species can sometimes been seen in gardens in countryside locations. The **yellowhammer** (*Emberiza citrinella*), the **corn bunting** (*Emberiza calandra*), **reed bunting** (*Emberiza schoeniclus*) and the **cirl bunting** (*Emberiza cirlus*) are all typical buntings. In the winter months these birds roam different habitats in search of food, including gardens.

Although rather dull in appearance, the house sparrow is often noticed because it has a noisy chirping call. *Melvin Yap*

The tree sparrow is told from the house sparrow by its chestnut coloured crown. *Melvin Yap*

Although similar in appearance to the other sparrows, the hedge sparrow is an insect eater rather than a seedeater. *Andrew*

Both the **house sparrow** (*Passer domesticus*) and the **tree sparrow** (*Passer montanus*) are seen in gardens, although the former is far more common than the latter and generally more comfortable living alongside humans. House sparrows have seen a steady decline in numbers over the past century, although this is really nothing more than an adjustment to changes in human technology. For one thing, farming techniques have improved in efficiency, so that seed and animal fodder are not spilled so often. Secondly, horses are no longer used for transportation and haulage, in town or country, so there is longer a supply of spilled oats, or part digested outs in horse droppings. So, house sparrow populations are really simply adjusting to the reduction in available food. In addition, the weatherboards and soffits on houses tend to be made of plastics that don't rot, so that fewer nesting holes are made available. House sparrows live in very localized colonies, so it is quite possible to see many in one street and none at all in an adjacent street. The **hedge sparrow** or dunnock (*Prunella modularis*) is not related to the other sparrows despite appearances. It is a skulking garden bird, usually seen on the ground or in undergrowth. It has a thin bill for eating insects. It is the only British representative of about a dozen bird species known as accentors.

Other species: Pipits (tree, meadow, rock), Larks (wood, sky).

TITS, GOLDCREST AND WREN

The **blue tit** (*Cyanistes caeruleus*), the **great tit** (*Parus major*), the **coal tit** (*Periparus ater*) and **long-tailed tit** (*Aegithalos caudatus*) are very familiar garden birds. They readily visit feeders and often nest in gardens. Their principal natural food is caterpillars, aphids and spiders, which they search

The blue tit is a familiar garden bird, that will readily come to feeders, and is particularly adept and hanging upside down. *Nick Goodrum*

The great tit is quite bossy towards other small birds and will often dominate a garden feeder until it has had its fill. *Sue Cro*

The coal tit is similar to the great tit in appearance, but its colours are more muted and it is also rather smaller. *Kentish Plumber*

The long-tailed tit is easily identified by its proportionately tail and its rounded body. *Kentish Plumber*

There is little to tell the willow tit (*left*) and the marsh tit (*below*) apart visually, but they do have different calls.

Katy Wrathall

Steve Herring

The goldcrest is a truly tiny bird that feeds primarily on small insects and spiders secreted among the needles of conifer trees. *Kentish Plumber*

The wren is adapted for hunting and feeding on invertebrates among the undergrowth and deadwood of woodland.

for on the foliage and branches of trees and shrubs. They are quite acrobatic in this regard, so they can exploit a food resource that is difficult to access for other birds. The first three species will often use bird boxes for nesting and for overnighting. The long-tailed tit builds a spherical nest from moss and cobwebs, in shrubs with dense protective foliage such as conifers and gorse. The **marsh tit** (*Poecile palustris*) and **willow tit** (*Poecile montanus*) are rather more dowdy in colour than the other tits. They are notoriously difficult to tell apart because they are so closely related that only their song is reliably diagnostic. The marsh tit is more common than the willow tit.

The **goldcrest** (*Regulus regulus*) is quite similar to the tits, as it too feeds on small invertebrates in the tree canopy. Its nest is also similar to that of the long-tailed tit, although it has an open top. The goldcrest is among a family of very small birds known as kinglets, as the colouring of the crest is reminiscent of a royal crown. In British gardens, it shares the title of smallest bird with the **wren** (*Troglodytes troglodytes*). It too, is insectivorous and builds a domed mossy nest, but the wren frequents the undergrowth in gardens, whilst the goldcrest frequents higher elevations.

Other species: crested tit, firecrest.

SWIFTS AND SWALLOWS

Just as bats harvest flying insects at night, so swifts and swallows do the same during the day. Unlike bats, these birds do not use echolocation to detect their prey, but eyesight. As a result, they have partial stereoscopic vision, so that they can judge distance. They then simply scoop insects from the air with their open mouths.

The **swift** (*Apus apus*) flies so fast that it has whiskers on the sides of its mouth to help with catching insects and to protect its eyes from injury. When in flight, the swift looks as though its wings are not synchronized. This is an optical illusion because the wings are so long and narrow. The bird is often seen in the skies above gardens, but it nests in the roof spaces of building such as churches, because they mimic the cliff and cave ledges they use in the wild. Although similar to the swift in design, the **swallow** (*Hirundo rustica*) and **house martin** (*Delichon urbicum*) are not related. They merely look similar to the swift because they have evolved to exploit the same airborne food resource. Swallows prefer to build their nests on beams and ledges in outbuildings, so they are more often found in rural gardens. House martins can build their nests to cantilever beneath the eaves of houses, so they often have colonies in suburban areas. They both construct composite nests from a mixture of dried mud and reinforcing fibres. The swift, swallow

The swallow (above) and the house martin (right) can often be seen gathering mud by the sides of ponds and streams for making their nests. *StefanBerndtsson*

Kentish Plumber

Although it looks similar to the swallow and the house martin, the swift is actually from a different family of birds.

Kentish Plumber

and house martin avoid direct competition for food by hunting at generally different altitudes. The swift is the high flyer, the swallow is the low flyer, with the house martin in between.

Other species: sand martin.

The cuckoo is a parasite of small songbirds, using their time and effort to feed and rear its own young. *Ron Knight*

CUCKOO

The **cuckoo** (*Cuculus canorus*) is notorious for its parasitic nesting behaviour. Instead of building its own nest and rearing its own offspring, the cuckoo has evolved to lay its eggs in the nest of other birds, where the young cuckoo is then fed by its foster parents. The adult cuckoo mimics the sparrowhawk, so the host birds fly for cover whilst the cuckoo lays its egg. The foster parents then become slaves to its appetite as the cuckoo chick grows larger than they are. This behaviour means that a female cuckoo can lay eggs in many host bird nests and therefore produce more young that it could otherwise do. Indeed, that is the very reason why natural selection favoured the parasitic behaviour, as it propagated a higher frequency of genes than conventional behaviour.

Cuckoos have become rather less commonly seen in gardens however, because their life history is reliant on healthy populations of host birds, which have also seen their populations reduced. Cuckoos specialize in eating the caterpillars of large moths, which have also declined in numbers, due to the use of pesticides and removal of unkempt habitat. All-in-all, the cuckoo is a casualty of the tidy and sterile modern garden and should be regarded as the litmus test of a genuinely healthy environment. Alas, its iconic 'cuck-oo' call has become something to be remarked upon rather than being a quintessential part of the British landscape, because so many ingredients need to be right for the cuckoo to flourish. For that reason, the RSPB should use the image of the cuckoo as its symbol of ambition, rather than the avocet, which says nothing about the British countryside.

GULLS

In recent years gulls have extended their range inland, in order to exploit the food waste in rural, suburban and urban areas. In the countryside, gulls will follow the plough in search of earthworms, in much the same way that they follow trawlers in search of chum. In suburban and urban areas, they use the flat roofs and chimneys as artificial ledges for nesting and they take advantage of the fast foods spilled onto pavements. When scraps are thrown onto a lawn, gulls can appear remarkably quickly because they circle the skies waiting for feeding opportunities. Intriguingly they cannot help but call when they find food, which then attracts other gulls, so they end up squabbling. This is an evolved behaviour to ensure that food is spread among the colony.

The **herring gull** (*Larus argentatus*) and the **lesser black-backed gull** (*Larus*

The herring gull *(left)* and the lesser black-backed gull *(right)* are very similar, but their backs are different shades of grey and they have different coloured legs.

fuscus) are two larger gulls species, and the **black headed gull** (*Chroicocephalus ridibundus*) and **common gull** (*Larus canus*) are two smaller species. All four can be seen scavenging in gardens, sometimes in mixed company. The term seagull is often used as a generic term for a gull, but there is no species with that name, in much the same way that the term cabbage white is used to describe several species of butterfly. Gulls have chicks that can already walk and have downy feathers for warmth when they hatch from their eggs. The term precocial is used for this kind of chick, while the term altricial is used to describe chicks that hatch naked and helpless, such as those of songbirds.

The common gull and the black-headed gull are relatively small species of gull.

GAME BIRDS

Another group of birds with precocial chicks is the game birds, so called because they are traditionally shot for food – the term game being used to describe wild meat. Most game birds are only seen in wild habitats, such as grouse, but a few species occasionally enter gardens in search of food. The **pheasant** (*Phasianus colchicus*), the **grey partridge** (*Perdix perdix*) and the **red-legged partridge** (*Alectoris rufa*) are all seen in gardens from time to time in search of birdseed, shoots and fallen fruit. The common partridge is native to Britain, while the other two have become naturalized, having been introduced for sport.

Other species: quail.

The male pheasant is a handsome bird, while the female is cryptically coloured for protection from predators whilst incubating eggs. *KevPBur*

The red-legged partridge *(above)* and common partridge *(below)* will sometimes forage in gardens, beneath bird tables.

vid Cook

Craig Adam

The coot *(left)* and moorhen *(right)* are both commonly found on larger ponds, where they are able to build their nests away from predators.

WATERFOWL

Waterfowl are not often seen in gardens unless there are bodies of water to attract them, such as large ponds or nearby rivers or streams. The most likely species to visit gardens are the **mallard duck** (*Anas platyrhynchos*), the **coot** (*Fulica atra*) and the **moorhen** (*Gallinula chloropus*). All three can be found in rural suburban and urban settings. Occasionally they will breed in gardens, but they require ponds big enough to enable them to build their nests safe from predators – protected by a moat of deep water.

Other species: mute swam, Canada goose, teal, snipe, woodcock, redshank.

The mallard is known as a dabbling duck, because it has the habit of dabbling the surface of water to wet its food. Kristie Gianopulos

REPTILES

There are very few reptiles in Britain and even fewer likely to be seen in gardens. In fact, there are just four species of snake and two species of lizard. Of the snakes, the **common grass-snake** (*Natrix natrix*) and the **barred grass snake** (*Natrix helvetica*) may be found in gardens. They are called grass snakes because they are attracted to the piles of grass cuttings in gardens, which heat up as the grass decomposes. Being ectothermic (cold blooded) this heat is a good place to warm up when the sun is obscured by clouds. It is also a good place to incubate eggs, as they develop more quickly.

Until recently, the common grass snake *(below)* and the barred grass snake *(right)* were treated as one species, but they are now considered to have enough difference to separated.

XulescuG

Bernard Dupont

The adder or viper will only bite if it feels threatened, so the best approach is to leave it alone. *Robert Shell*

Grass snakes feed primarily on frogs, toads and newts, so they are particularly attracted to gardens that include ponds. It is also possible to attract them with sheets of corrugated iron, as they enjoy the warmth that builds up below, enabling them to bask without feeling vulnerable. When caught, grass snakes defecate to produce an extremely unpleasant smell, clearly designed to deter predators.

The **adder or viper** (*Vipera berus*) is the only venomous British reptile. Its bite is seldom fatal, but best avoided anyway, as it is certainly painful. Adders are occasionally found in gardens adjacent to their natural habitat, which is heathland and copse, but they usually shy away when they detect the vibration of footsteps. Although they will use their venom for defence, they are always reluctant to waste it, because it is far more useful for killing their prey, which comprises small mammals and birds.

The **common lizard** (*Lacerta vivipara*) is also found in some gardens. It particularly likes dry stone walling and rockeries, where there are plenty of places to hide and nest. They bask on the stone surfaces and live in small colonies. The common lizard is fairly unusual in being ovoviviparous, meaning that the female retains her eggs in the body until they hatch, so that she gives

The common lizard lives in small colonies in suitable places, such as dry-stone walls and on heathland. *Tony Morris*

birth to live young. This is the secret to their success in temperate climates, as it means that they can keep their eggs warm enough to incubate. Common lizards feed on a variety of small invertebrates.

Other species: smooth snake, sand lizard.

AMPHIBIANS

All British amphibians require water in which to reproduce, but they can be found surprising distances from water during the rest of the year. When they are found in gardens without ponds, it indicates that there is probably a pond within half a mile or so. They need to spread out in order to establish territories for hunting, so they find suitably damp places to hide during the day and look for prey under cover of darkness. The **common frog** (*Rana temporaria*) and **common toad** (*Bufo bufo*) are both well-known garden animals. The toad has a dryer and thicker skin than the frog, so it is able to cope with dryer conditions, so they avoid looking for prey in the same places.

The **smooth newt** (*Lissotriton vulgaris*), the **palmate newt** (*Lissotriton helveticus*) and the **crested newt** (*Triturus cristatus*) can all be found in gardens. They vary in distribution and rarity, but can all be common in the right places. Sometime two or all three species are found in the same habitat. Frogs lay their eggs as masses of spawn and toads lay them in strings, while newts lay them individually on the leaves of pondweed. Young newts are known as efts and are sometimes found beneath rocks in gardens, looking like small rubber toys.

Other species: edible frog, natterjack toad.

The common frog is extremely variable in its patterns and colours, ranging from greens, to browns to reds.

The common toad is usually encountered hiding underneath objects in the garden when they are being moved.

rentLebois

S Rae

For most of the year the great crested newt has no crest and looks rather like a black glossy lizard. *Mike Lane*

Holger Leyrer

The smooth newt *(above)* and the palmate newt *(below)* are smaller than the great crested newt and have generally paler colours.

Mike Lane

FISH

Of course, it is unusual for gardens to include wild species of fish, but as a few gardens have streams running through them, or alongside them, some small fish species qualify as 'garden fish'. As streams and brooks tend to be shallow and relatively fast flowing, they are home to only a few species of fish, as well as the fry and juveniles of larger fish species. Furthermore, such streams can flow through rural, suburban and urban areas, so fish can survive in them as long as the quality of the water is good enough. These stream fish cannot survive in small bodies of standing water, such as garden ponds, as they require flowing water to provide enough oxygen.

The classic stream fish are the **three-spined stickleback** (*Gasterosteus aculeatus*), the **minnow** (*Phoxinus phoxinus*), the **bullhead** (*Cottus gobio*) and

The minnow is the quintessential stream fish, seen swimming in shoals in shallow water. *Scott Wilson*

The gudgeon is a bottom-feeder, preying on various invertebrates living in the mud and gravel. *Giles San Martin*

The bullhead has a disproportionately large head and mouth for gulping prey in one go. *Hans Hillewaert*

The eel travels out to sea for several years before returning to our rivers having reached adulthood. *Anna Barnett*

the **gudgeon** (*Gobio gobio*). These are the fish commonly caught by children in nets and placed in jam-jars for close scrutiny. There are two more primitive fish found in streams too. They are the **eel** (*Anguilla anguilla*) and the river **lamprey** (*Lampetra fluviatilis*). As they are long and thin, they can survive in shallow water when quite large. The lamprey is a parasitic fish, with a toothed sucker-mouth for draining the blood of larger fish. The other species feed primarily on aquatic invertebrates.

INVERTEBRATES

D ue to their diminutive size, invertebrates account for the vast majority of individual animals in any garden, as they inhabit all of the nooks and crannies that each microhabitat has to offer. It pays to realize that invertebrates are not really aware of the existence of humanity, as their senses are attuned to their own world and concerns – finding food, avoiding predators and reproduction. So they go about their lives unaware that we are watching them, as we typically play no part in their existence. In fact, they usually only react to our presence if we present a threat to their survival, so that instinct makes them react by fleeing or defending themselves when they sense danger. Of course, a few species also pester us because we present a food source to them; either by way of our blood or by the different foodstuffs we bring into their garden environment.

One of the remarkable things about invertebrates is their resilience. They virtually disappear during the winter months, yet they reappear in armies as soon as the weather becomes more congenial in the springtime. They have been doing the same thing year-in year-out for billennia, as they evolved long before humans existed and they will doubtless continue their occupation of the planet long after humans have become the authors of their own demise. They are so well adapted for their different walks of life that most have changed very little over tens of millions of years. There are ants and beetles fossilized in amber, for example, that look virtually identical to their living counterparts. Natural selection has no need to modify the design of a species if it does the job perfectly well already, so most invertebrates are 'living fossils' – unchanged and unaltered since time immemorial. We, on the other hand, are still a short-lived experiment.

INSECTS

In terms of species, the insects are the most numerous invertebrates in our gardens. In America they are called *bugs*, but this is misleading, as the term *bug* is reserved for a certain order of insects. All insects have three body parts (head, thorax, abdomen) and three pairs of legs. Some types of insect undergo complete metamorphosis, so that the larva, the pupa and the adult look different from one another. Others undergo partial metamorphosis, so that the nymph looks similar to the adult form and gradually changes. Most insects are solitary, but a few are eusocial; meaning that a queen is served by workers. Genetically, the workers are more closely related to one another than they would be to their own offspring, so they instinctively work for the greater good of the colony. This is known as *haplodiploidy*.

In effect, insects have their own miniature world, where some species are herbivores, some are carnivores and others are omnivores. When they evolved, there were few other terrestrial animals, so they filled all of the econiches available to them. That dynamic has remained between them even though higher organisms have since evolved with similar dynamics. If we consider fish, amphibians, reptiles, birds and mammals, they all have similar worlds, with herbivores, carnivores and omnivores. So there are layers of organisms that make up an ecosystem, with many interconnections. By and large, insects survive by having high rates of reproduction. For example; if two insects produce a hundred offspring, then only two offspring need to survive to keep the insect population stable. Therefore, they can afford to lose ninety-eight offspring without it making a difference to their surviving population. It is this strategy that has kept insects part of life on earth despite the evolution of other animals that rely of them as a source of food.

BEETLES (Coleoptera)

In our gardens, beetles range in size from tiny flea beetles to the spectacular **stag beetle**, with many shapes and size in between. Beetles have chewing mouthparts and modified front wings, called elytra, that provide protective armour. They also undergo complete metamorphosis.

The dor beetle is a type of dung beetle. Its name alludes to the loud sound it makes in flight, as dor is a Mediaeval word for a bumblebee. Gerard Cheshire

Alison Day

The wasp beetle *(left)* and the hornet longhorn beetle *(right)*. Gerard Cheshire

The stag beetle *(left)* and lesser stag beetle *(right)* have larvae that feed in the rotting stumps and fallen trunks of large trees. Gerard Cheshire

The glow-worm is a type of beetle that feeds on snails, and is able to emit a bright greenish light for communication at night. Gerard Cheshire

Ian Boyd

The garden chafer, cock chafer and rose chafer all have larvae that feed on the roots of garden plants. *Gerard Cheshire*

The black ground-beetle *(left)* and the violet ground-beetle *(above)* both hunt for prey among the sward of lawns and the humus in flowerbeds. *Gerard Cheshire*

In a typical garden there are particular types of beetle that predominate. Among others, there are ground beetles, leaf beetles, flea beetles, ladybirds, chafers, wood-boring beetles, soldier beetles, rove beetles, click beetles, burying beetles, longhorn beetles, weevils and water beetles. Others, such as dung beetles, glowworms, tiger beetles and oil beetles, require more specific habitats. Beetles inhabit all levels of garden habitat, from the soil to the canopy of trees. Some are nocturnal, while others are diurnal. Some eat leaves, whilst others hunt other insects and invertebrates, and still others scavenge in detritus.

The black weevil is typical of the many species of weevil, having an elongated snout, rounded body and gripping feet. *Gerard Cheshire*

Giles San Martin

Gerard Cheshire

The spangled diving beetle is among several species that live in water as larvae and adults.

The bloody-nosed beetle emits a noxious fluid to deter predators, which is reddish in colour and reminiscent of blood.

Judy Gallagher

Gail Hampshire

Gail Hampshire

The soldier beetle, sailor beetle and cardinal beetle have their names because they reminded people of various brightly coloured costumes.

The carrion beetle, or burying beetle, feeds on the carcasses of small mammals and birds, and therefore smells of rotting flesh. *Kentish Plumber*

Ladybirds come in a variety of sizes, patterns and colour combinations – 2-spot, 7-spot, 11-spot, and so on. The designs are known as aposematic colouration and warn birds that they taste unpleasant.

Among the most popular of garden beetles are the ladybirds, mainly due to their bright cartoon colours. Ladybirds are favoured by gardeners too, as they prey upon aphids – often known as greenfly and blackfly. Ladybirds come in a variety of sizes and colour combinations. This is known as aposematic colouring, as it is designed to deter birds from trying to eat them. Any child will know that ladybirds also exude an orange fluid, which smells something like peanuts. This tastes unpleasant to birds, so they spit the beetles out and then learn to avoid the bright colours by association.

BUGS (Hemiptera)

Bugs are often mistaken for beetles, as they can look rather similar, but they are different in some important ways. For one thing, bugs have sucking mouthparts instead of chewing jaws. Secondly, their elytra (wing cases) are leathery and flat rather than hard and rounded. Thirdly, bugs develop as nymphs that look similar to the adults, rather than larvae.

The common froghopper uses camouflage, while the red-black leafhopper uses mimicry.

Gail Hampshire

The green shield-bug and mauve shield-bug are often seen flying around gardens and landing on bushes.

Strange Ones

Charlie Jackson

Peter O'Connor

Christophe Quintin

The yellow plant-bug and the red plant-bug are walking bugs, as they have fairly long legs.

Having sucking mouthparts restricts the diet of bugs to fluids. As a result, some bugs drink the sap of plants, while others drink the fluids of other animals. Garden bugs include shield bugs, leaf bugs, plant hoppers, aphids, plant lice and water bugs. Bugs found in ponds are carnivorous as they prey on flying insects that fall into the water. A few terrestrial species, known as assassin bugs, have a long proboscis for attacking other animals. Most bugs feed on the juices of plants in one way or another – sap from the stems, nectar from the flowers, juice from the fruits.

The most abundant garden bugs are the aphids, found on the succulent growth of plants. Aphids reproduce asexually, which means that females

The reduvius and coranus assassin bugs have piercing mouthparts for sucking the fluids of other insects.

atmeg66

Gail Hampshire

Wikimedia Commons

Wolfram Sonderman

Sam Dredge

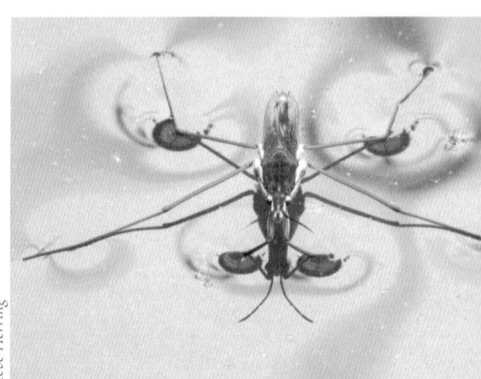
Steve Herring

The water scorpion *(top left)*, water stick-insect *(top right)*, water boatman *(left)* and pond-skater *(right)* are all bugs that hunt for their prey in aquatic environments.

Green aphids are often called greenfly, while black aphids are called blackfly.

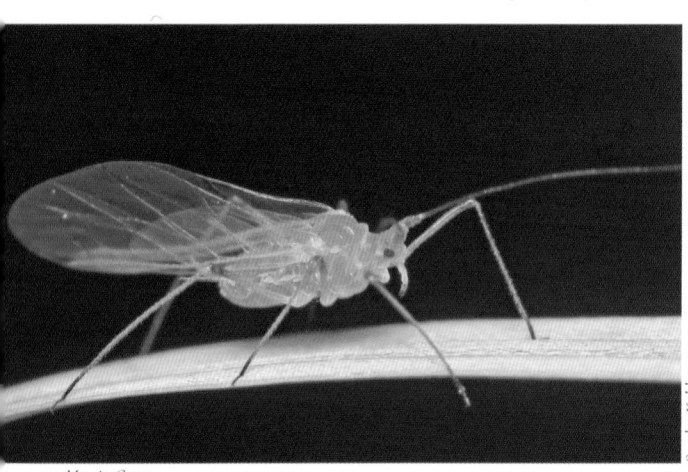
Martin Cooper

Sascha Kohlmann

simply produce clones of themselves without mating. Furthermore, they give birth to live young, so they can multiply very rapidly to take advantage of an abundance of food. The only drawback is a lack of genetic variety, so they mate with male aphids later in the year. Aphids have an evolved association with ants. This is a symbiotic relationship, whereby the ants protect the aphids from predators in exchange for honeydew, which is a sugary secretion derived from the sap and much beloved by the ants. As aphids are preyed upon by ladybirds, hoverflies, lacewings, and so on, the ants herd the aphids together and stand on sentry duty, ready to tackle any intruders. It has been likened to a shepherd protecting his flock of sheep from wolves. The cicadas that we hear on holiday in the Mediterranean are also bugs. They are basically giant-sized plant hoppers. Their nymphs feed on sap from the roots of trees and ferns by burrowing through the soil. They take several years to reach maturity, so there are always several generations in the ground when a new season of adults emerges. In Britain there is just one species of cicada, found only rarely in the New Forest.

FLIES (Diptera)

Many insects are described as flies, but true flies are distinguished by having just one pair of wings instead of two pairs. In fact, the second pair have been reduced in size to tiny baton like structures called halteres. There is an evolutionary tradeoff here, as having one pair of wings enables more complex flight, but the halteres are needed to enhance the insect's sense of balance and orientation. It is most perfectly seen in the hoverflies, which are able to

The fruit-fly and the yellow dung-fly both have larvae that feed on decomposing vegetable matter – rotting fruit and the dung of herbivores.

Christophe Quintin

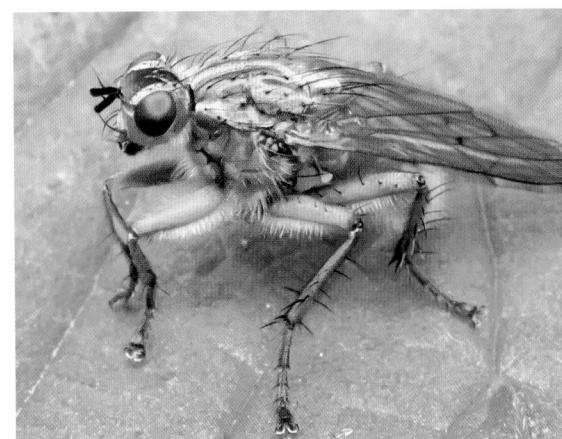

Derek Parker

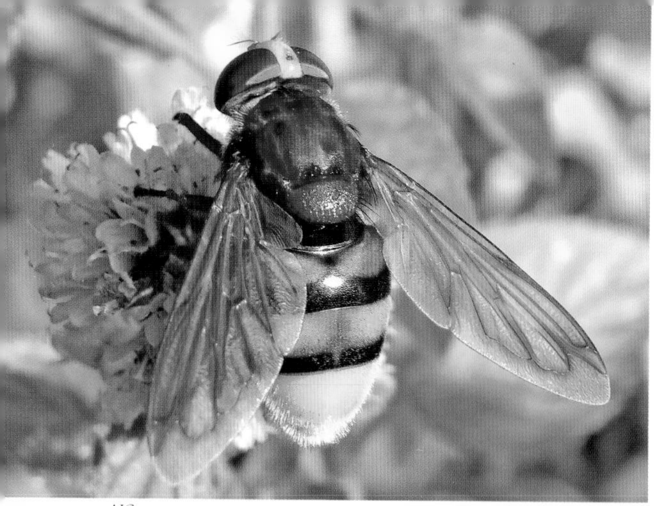

AJC1

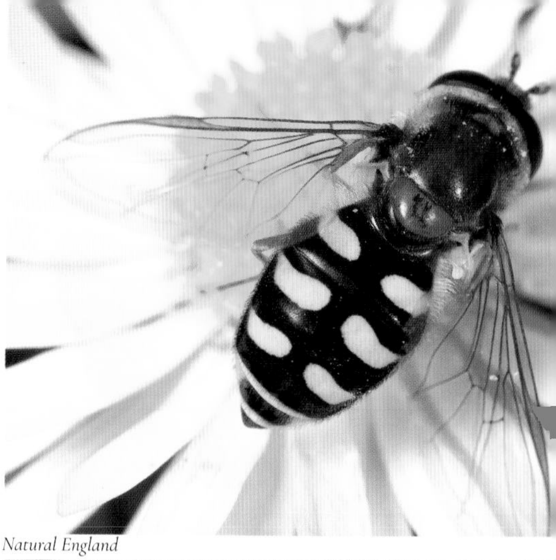

Natural England

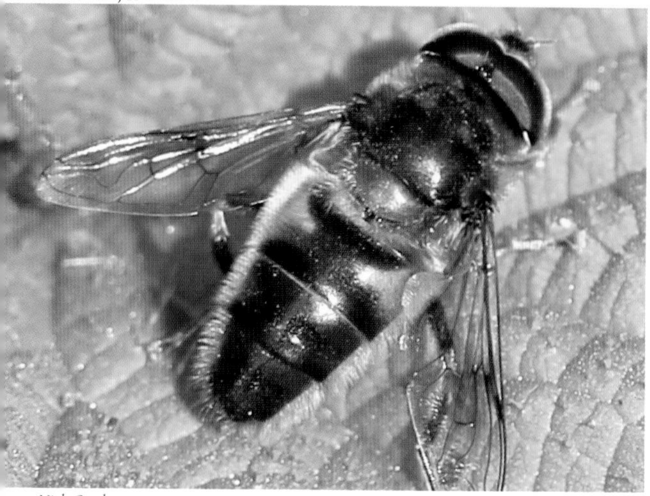

Nick Goodrum

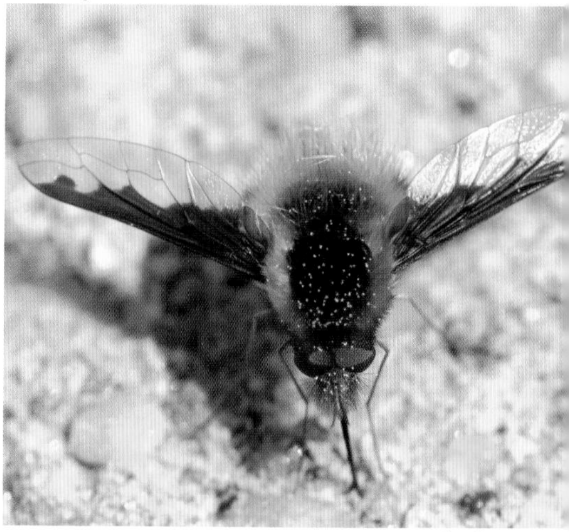

John Flannery

The volucella fly *(top left)*, the hoverfly *(top right)*, the drone fly *(bottom left)* and the bee fly *(bottom right)* have evolved to mimic the hornet, the wasp the honey bee and the bumble bee, as a form of protection from predatory birds.

The blue bottle, green bottle and flesh-fly are known as blow flies, because their larvae feed on rotting carcasses, which are said to be 'blown' with maggots.

John Flannery

Line Sabroe

Frank Vassen

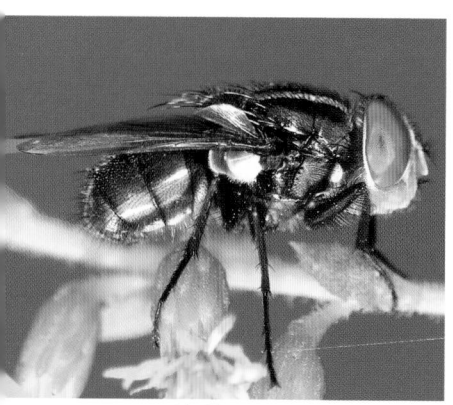

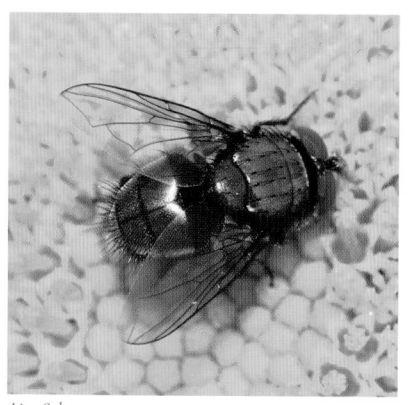

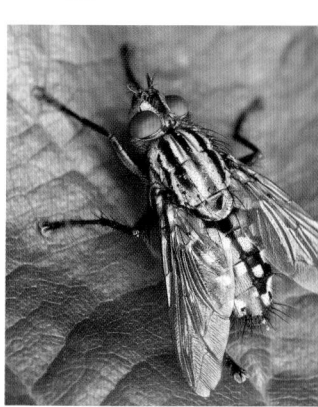

perform impressive aerobatics and reversing. In the case of craneflies, they have subsequently evolved to become clumsy fliers despite the sophisticated flight of their ancestors.

Garden flies include blowflies, hoverflies, craneflies, flesh flies, mosquitoes, gnats, bee flies, horseflies, stable flies and fruit flies. Some species have piercing mouthparts for sucking blood, while others have proboscis designed for sucking up fluids, including the digestive juices that the flies use to dissolve substances. Flies develop as larvae, often described as maggots, which typically feed on decaying plant or animal matter. Others feed on live prey. The **fruit fly** – *Drosophila melanogaster* – has become well known in scientific laboratories as a demonstrator or genetic and evolutionary theory. In gardens it infests fallen fruit and plays a key role in the recycling of nutrients. Its

The **horse fly** (*below*), **stable fly** (*right*), **mosquito** (*bottom left*) **and gnat** (*bottom right*) have piercing mouthpart for feeding on the blood of mammals, which includes humans.

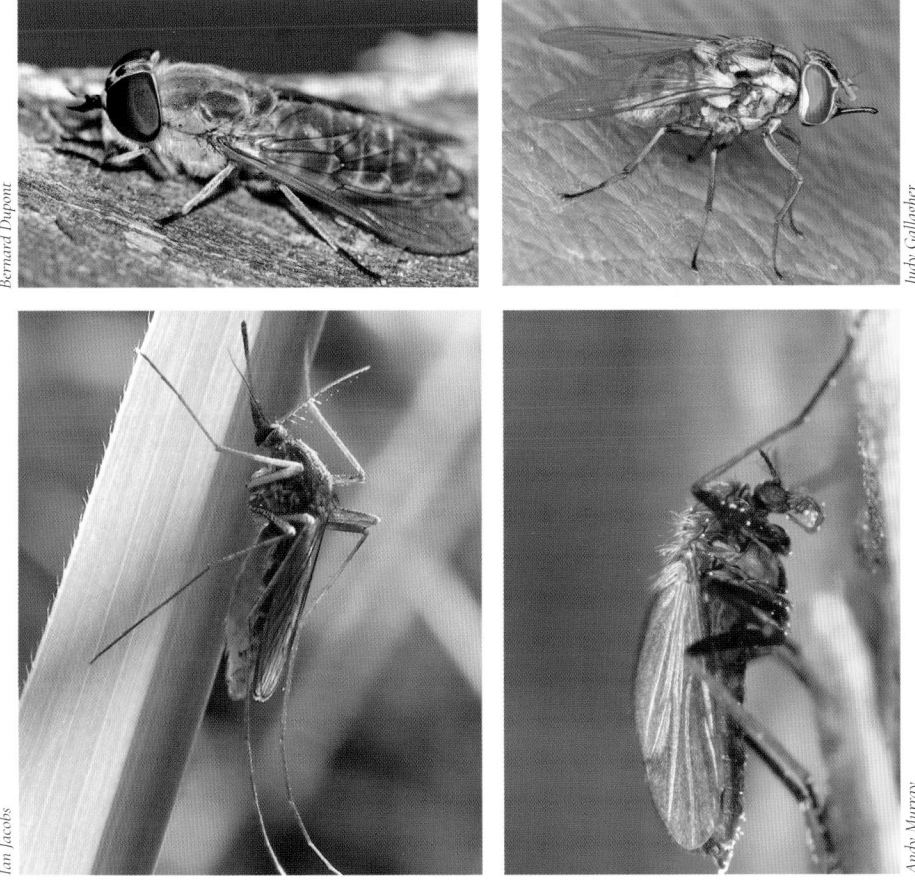

Despite its large size and appearance, the crane-fly does not have working mouthparts and is entirely harmless to humans. *Chris Cooper*

The robber fly feeds by attacking other flying insects from above and then sucking out their body fluids. *GBohne*

scientific name means *lover of dross* (waste). The hoverflies are conspicuous in gardens because they mimic the appearance of wasps and bees for protection from predators. They are often so convincing that people will duck and dive for fear of being stung. However, hoverflies are perfectly harmless. Blowflies are responsible for the masses of white maggots found in bins and on rotting meat. Although this usually repulses people, it should be remembered that sterilized blowfly maggots are very effective at cleaning infected wounds in hospitals.

GRASSHOPPERS AND CRICKETS (Orthoptera)

Most gardens have grasshoppers and crickets of one kind or another. In fact, there are a few distinct groups: ground crickets, bush crickets, grasshoppers and ground hoppers. As a general rule, grasshoppers and ground hoppers have short antennae and are vegetarian, while crickets have long antennae and are omnivorous. They all develop as nymphs, so they tend to be

The common green, field and meadow grasshoppers look similar to one another, but they all have relatively short antennae compared with crickets.

Chris Parker

Kentish Plumber

Nutmeg66

Gerard Cheshire

The oak and speckled bush-crickets have relatively long antennae compared with grasshoppers.

inconspicuous until they reach adulthood, when they can sing and fly. Their eggs are laid in the ground or in plants. In the case of bush crickets, the females are typically equipped with a sword-like ovipositor, which they use to split plant stems in order to lay their eggs.

Grasshoppers are popular food for birds, so they are well camouflaged, both in colouring and shape, so that they can hide among grass blades. Sometimes many hundreds will fly up from the sward when someone walks across a lawn. They prefer long grass, so it is always good to leave a patch uncut to encourage them. Grasshoppers sing, or stridulate, during the day, as

The wood cricket is a type of ground living or true cricket that lives in a burrow.
Gail Hampshire

they are diurnal. Crickets tend to sing in the evenings and at night, as they are usually nocturnal. Stridulation is achieved by the insects rubbing two parts of their bodies together in a similar way to the thumbnail running across the teeth of a comb. Grasshoppers rub their legs against their wings, whilst crickets rub their wings together. They sing to communicate and find mates. There is a peculiar member of this order of insects called the mole cricket. It is not a garden species as it burrows in the soft damp soil of riverbanks on floodplains. As its name suggests, it is reminiscent of the mole, as it has greatly enlarged front legs for digging and is dark brown in colour. Rarely among non-social insects, the female mole cricket protects its young in a nest for a while before allowing them to leave and fend for themselves.

ANTS, WASPS, BEES AND SAWFLIES: (Hymenoptera)

Many species of ant, wasp and bee are eusocial, which means that they live in close-knit social colonies. They are described as *eusocial* rather than *social*, because the genetics of the workers compels them to dedicate their lives for the greater good of the colony without any prospect of reproducing themselves. In other social species it is possible to climb through the ranks and potentially pass on one's own genes.

Christophe Quintin

AJCi

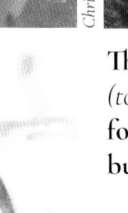

The black ant *(top left)*, meadow ant *(top right)* and red ant *(left)* are all found on garden lawns, where they buid their nests below ground.

Fractality

In wasp and bee species, except the honeybee, only the queens survive the winter, while the workers and drones (males) die off. Honeybee colonies are able to survive because they store their own winter fuel. This is the honey that humans like to eat and the reason why colonies are collected from the wild and kept in hives. In the wild they usually nest in trees cavities.

The wood ant is found in garden where there are pine trees, as it like to use the needles for constructing its nest, which takes the form of a mound. *Christophe Quintin*

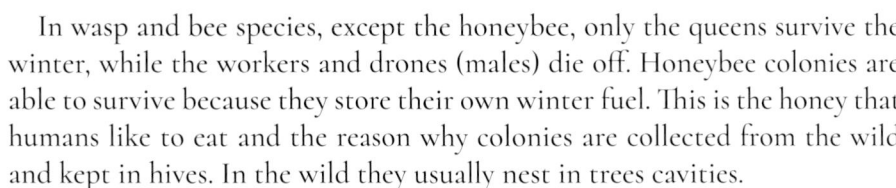

In our gardens there are usually two groups of ants: *Myrmica* species and Lasius species. *Myrmica* are the red ants, of which there are several very similar species. Lasius are the black ants and the yellow or meadow ants. *Myrmica* ants live in colonies beneath lawns and are spaced out to give each colony a territory for finding food. Black ants tend to live in cavities below paths and patios, from where they go on relatively long journeys in search of food; often entering houses. Meadow ants prefer long grass meadow where they build mounds from the excavated soil. The grass stems provide reinforcement within the mounds to prevent them from collapsing. Although red ants will give a mild sting when people inadvertently sit on their nests, they are otherwise quite harmless, as are black and meadow ants. Some people find black ants a nuisance when they scout kitchens in search of sweet foods, but they don't present a hygiene risk. The fact that they go out of their way to find sugary substances tells us that sugars are a rare and valuable commodity in the wild. This is why plants use sugars in their flowers and fruits to provide the incentive for animals to fertilize them and to spread their seeds. In order for the females and males of different ant colonies to mate and maintain gene flow, there are coordinated days when many virgin 'queens' and 'kings' take to the air in search of mates. These nuptial flights are triggered by dry and warm weather conditions, so that all of the nests erupt with synchronicity. In the vernacular these are known as 'flying ant days'. As soon as the queen ants have copulated they remove their wings and search for potential nesting sites. The vast majority of these ants are not successful, as only one queen from each colony needs to establish a new nest to keep the ant population stable. In fact, queen ants can live for as long as thirty years, and they only need one successful daughter and son during their lifetime. The odds may therefore be as low as one in a million. Many flying ants become food for birds, which can often be seen apparently snapping at the air high above our gardens, or else pecking at the ground. In effect, flying ants are on a suicide mission as their chances of success are so very slim. Indeed, all males die anyway, so only their genes have the potential to survive if they happen to mate with a lucky queen from another colony.

Most eusocial wasps and bumblebees build their nests in dry cavities of a suitable size and with restricted access to keep predators away. Such cavities may be found in trees, in old rabbit burrows or in the roof spaces of houses. Bumblebee nests are made of wax derived from pollen and are usually quite modest in size. Wasps build their nests from papier-mâché derived from wood and can often grow to house thousands of insects. As wasps tend to aggressively defend their nests then it is appropriate to have their nests removed if they present a problem in gardens. Our largest wasp, the hornet, is

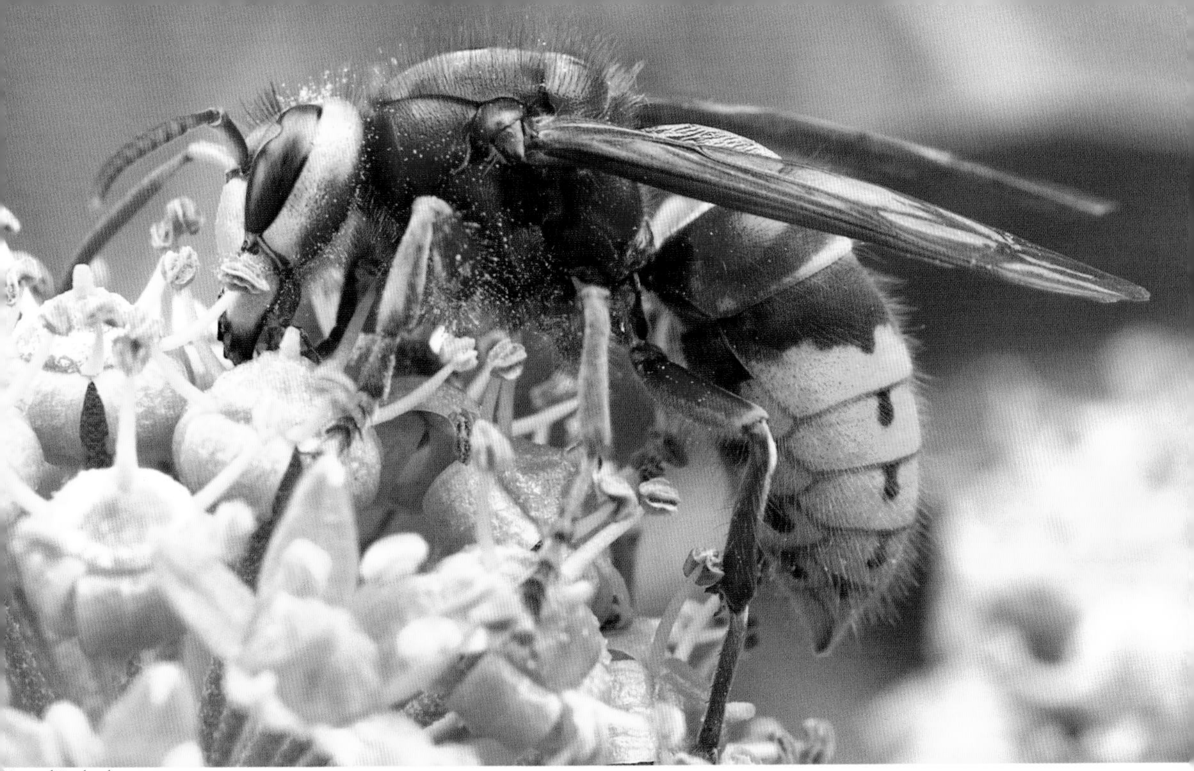

Natural England

OmageAurochs

Gail Hampshire

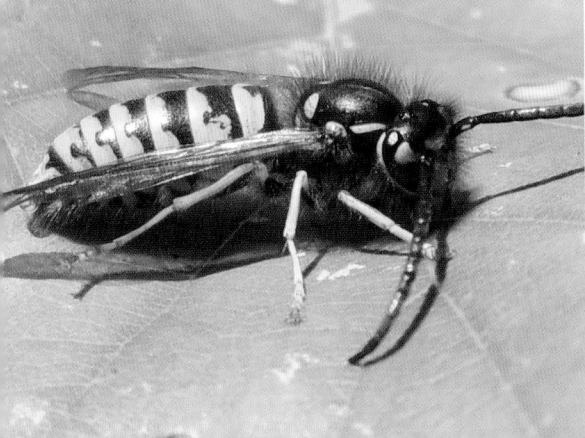

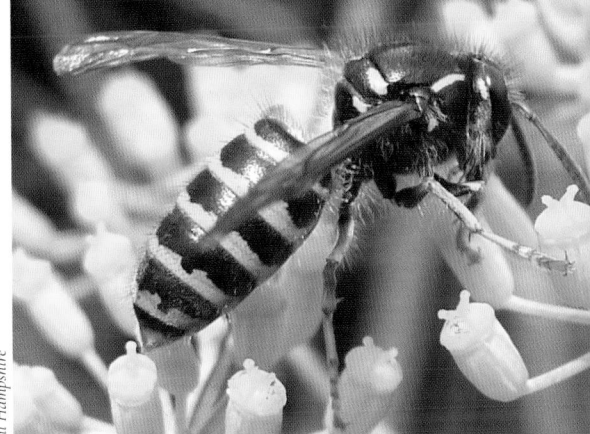

The hornet ***(top)*** **is larger and browner in colour than the common wasp** ***(left)*** **and the tree wasp** ***(right)*****.**

not an aggressive species despite its formidable appearance.

Not all wasps and bees are eusocial. Many species are solitary and do not build communal nests. These include leafcutter bees, mining bees, digging bees, sweat bees, parasitic wasps, spider hunting wasps, caterpillar hunting wasps, ichneumon wasps and gall wasps. Velvet ants are also solitary, but they are actually wingless wasps, rather than ants.

Sawflies are unusual relatives of ants, bees and wasps. Their larvae resemble caterpillars with curled tails, and their presence in gardens is evident when

The white-tailed bumblebee is often seen in gardens and is one of various species with different colour combinations. *Mark Robinson*

they have stripped the foliage of garden plants. An example is the rose sawfly, whose larvae are known colloquially as rose worms or rose slugs. The name sawfly alludes to the saw-like ovipositor that the female uses to cut into plant stems or wood for laying her eggs; sometimes mistaken for a sting. Wood wasps are large species of sawfly that inject their eggs into the wood-boring larvae of beetles and moths. Sawflies often have similar markings to wasps, but they lack the narrow waistline. Nor can sawflies sting, which is why they mimic their cousins, for protection.

The larvae of the rose sawfly and the green sawfly looks very similar to caterpillars, but they have curled tails and have a glassy appearance. *Nikk*

DRAGONFLIES AND DAMSELFLIES (Odonata)

The names 'dragonfly' and 'damselfly' evoke quite different Mediaeval perceptions of these insects. One is seen as a robust and aggressive monster, the other a dainty and passive creature. In fact, both are voracious hunters of other flying insects.

Dragonflies and damselflies are told apart by a couple of fundamental physical details. Apart from being generally more heavily built than damselflies, dragonflies rest with their wings outstretched, rather than folded behind their backs. In addition, the eyes of dragonflies wrap around their heads, whilst those of damselflies are widely positioned left and right. This is because dragonflies and damselflies hunt in different ways. Dragonflies hunt by either patrolling on the wing, or by using lookout posts. Their eyes enable them to spot prey stereoscopically in a hemisphere in front of them, so they can accurately pursue their quarry. Damselflies tend to perch among the foliage of trees and shrubs, so folding their wings keeps them out of harm's way. Their eyes are positioned to see only monoscopically, but with a wide arc each side, so they have a greater combined field of vision even though they cannot judge distance so well. Thus, dragonflies and damselflies use slightly different

The emperor (*top left*), southern hawker (*above right*) and golden-ringed dragonflies (*left*) are three of the very large species that can be seen hunting along garden margins in late summer.
Paul Ritchie

The common darter is a small dragonfly often seen in gardens, using plants as lookout posts for hunting prey. The male is reddish and the female is greenish. *Jerry Hoare*

hunting techniques. When dragonflies take to the air, they flap their wings with a shallow draught and glide in between. Damselflies flap their wings with a deep draught, more like a butterfly, as their wings are not rigid and wide enough for gliding. The two also tend to catch different types of insect prey, so they avoid direct competition with one another. Both dragonflies

The banded agrion and the demoiselle are two large species of damselfly. They always rest with their wings folded behind. *Gerard Cheshire*

Dlougs

The azure *(above)*, **common blue** *(below left)* and **blue-tailed** *(below right)* are typical small species of damselfly, often seen flying in tall grass in gardens. *Gerard Cheshire*

and damselflies produce nymphs that develop in still or slow-moving water, so they need ponds, canals and rivers for breeding. However, they do roam some distance from water as adults, so they are often seen in gardens without ponds or any water nearby. Their nymphs are also predatory, feeding on other aquatic animals. They have extendable lower jaws for reaching their prey, which is then pulled towards the mouth. The nymphs take two or three years to develop, but the adults live for just a few weeks.

BUTTERFLIES AND MOTHS (Lepidoptera)

It seems fair to say that butterflies are the most popular insects in any garden, as they are quite harmless and they bring a splash of colour on sunny days as they flit from one flower to the next.

The patterns and colours on the wings of butterflies and moths are created by thousands of scales, much like a mosaic. They first evolved as a defence from predators, as the scales detach very easily, making the wings slippery when birds attempt to catch them in their beaks. Since then, the scales have developed patterns and colours for various reasons. Firstly, many species are camouflaged, so that they effectively disappear when they land on an appropriate background. Secondly, they help butterflies identify others of their own species and to distinguish between males and females. Thirdly, some species use their markings as a kind of dazzle mechanism to confuse predators and imitate flowers. Fourthly, some colour combinations deter predators because they are associated with toxins and stings in other insects – they are called aposematic colouring.

The colours of the scales are achieved in two ways. Firstly, there are pigment colours, much like the colours in a paint box. Secondly, there are structural colours, which means that they diffract white light to produce iridescent colours from particular angles. Often, both pigment colours and structural colours are used in combination, so that the iridescence appears as a metallic sheen over the pigmentation. Beneath the scales, the wing is a lightweight transparent membrane with strengthening veins. Distinguishing between butterflies and moths is not as clear-cut as one may think. Although most moths are nocturnal and most butterflies are diurnal, there are species that break the rule. Many moths fly in daylight, and a few butterflies continue flying at dusk. What about other ways to tell them apart? When at rest, typical butterflies fold their wings together behind their backs, while typical moths leave them spread-eagle. Again though, there are exceptions to the rule. A third approach is to look at the antennae. Typical butterflies have club-shaped tips to their antennae, while typical moths have tapering or feathered antennae. Again, there are exceptions to the rule. A fourth method is to look at their pupae. Typical moth pupae are generic in appearance; brown and rounded, because they are enclosed in a cocoon. Butterfly pupae are camouflaged and either hang upside down, or they are cantilevered in an upright position and held by a silk girdle. There are exceptions to this rule too.

So, in truth there is no reliable diagnostic difference between butterflies and moths. In other words, in biological terms, they are not separate clades because there are transitional species that span the gap between typical

Brimstone.

Clouded Yellow.

Small White.

Large White (*female*).

Green Veined White.

Orange Tip.

These butterflies all belong to the Pieridae – otherwise known as whites and yellows. *Gerard Cheshire*

Small Heath.

Hedge Brown. *Nick Goodr*

Speckled Wood.

Marbled White

Wall Butterfly.

Ringlet.

Meadow Brown.

These butterflies all belong to the Satyridae – otherwise known as browns.
Gerard Cheshire

Common Blue.

Holly Blue.

Small Copper.

Brown Argus.

Purple Hairstreak.
Don Sutherland

White-letter
Hairstreak.
Helen M Bushe

These butterflies all belong to the Lycaenidae – otherwise known as blues,
coppers and hairstreaks. *Gerard Cheshire*

Comma.

Small Tortoiseshell.

Red Admiral.

Peacock.

Adam Powell

Adobe Stock

Painted Lady.

Silver-washed Fritillary.

These butterflies all belong to the Nymphalidae – otherwise known as vanessids and fritillaries. *Gerard Cheshire*

butterflies and moths. Despite this, for the sake of convenience there are families of Lepidoptera described as either butterflies or moths.

The common garden butterflies belong to the following families: *Pieridae* contains the white and yellow butterflies. *Lycaenidae* contains the blues, coppers and hairstreaks. *Hesperiidae* contains the skippers. *Nymphalidae* includes sub-families: *Nymphalinae* contains the red admiral, small tortoiseshell, peacock, painted lady; *Satyrinae* contains the browns and heaths; *Heliconlinae* contains the woodland fritillaries.

The common moth families are as follows: *Sphingidae* contains the hawkmoths; *Noctuidae* contains the typical and underwing moths; *Zygaenidae* contains the burnet and forester moths; *Geometridae* contains the looper, inchworm and delta-wing moths; *Drepanidae* contains the hook-tip moths; *Sesiidae* contains the hornet mimic and clearwing moths; *Notodontidae* contains the prominent and kitten moths; *Erebidae* contains the tiger and ermine moths; *Lasiocampidae* contains the eggar moths; *Hepialidae* contains

Large Skipper.

Small Skipper.

Essex Skipper.

These butterflies all belong to the Hesperiidae – otherwise known as skippers. *Gerard Cheshire*

Eyed Hawk.

Hummingbird Hawk.

Large Elephant Hawk.

Small Elephant Hawk.

Lime Hawk.

Poplar Hawk.

The hawk moths are large and strongly built moths, hence their name, as they have wings that remind people of hawks.

Gerard Cheshire

Privet Hawk.

Jersey Tiger.

Ruby Tiger.

Cream-Spot Tiger. *Brian Wingent*

Scarlet Tiger.

Garden Tiger.

The tiger moths are some of the most colourful moths seen in British gardens.
Gerard Cheshire

the swift moths; *Cossidae* contains the wood-boring moths.

Just about every native British plant is food to the caterpillars of at least one species of butterfly or moth, so it is always a good idea to allow 'weeds' to grow and flourish in our gardens. Conversely, most cultivars are either foreign plants or they are genetically changed so much from their native forms that they are not suitable food plants. By-and-large, the plants we acquire from garden centres may look nice to the human eye, but they are not attractive to

Orange Underwing.

Red Underwing.

Yellow Underwing.

Blue Underwing.

57Andrew

The 'underwing' moths are so called because they have brightly coloured hind wings, which are usually covered by their cryptically marked forewings. *Gerard Cheshire*

our butterflies and moths, except perhaps as sources of nectar for the adults.

It used to be the case that people collected butterflies and moths, pinned in cabinets. These days there is no reason for doing so, as digital photography has reached a point where it is far more ethically acceptable to collect photographs instead. It is worth saying also, that some relatively inexpensive cameras are just as good at capturing high quality images in the right hands. It merely takes practice and patience, as digital technology allows the photographer to see the results instantly and then improve upon their images on the spot.

Angle-shades Moth.

Lappet Moth.

Bufftip

These moths all rely on camouflage to conceal their whereabouts from predatory birds. *Gerard Cheshire*

Lobster Moth.

Peppered Moth.

OTHER INSECTS

There are a few other insect orders found in British gardens, but with relatively few species. *Dictyoptera* contains the cockroaches. In the natural setting there are a few species generally known as wood cockroaches. Their name is a corruption of the Spanish name: *cucaracha*. They are smaller and paler in colour than the cockroaches associated with indoor environments. *Dermaptera* contains the earwigs. Their name is a contraction of 'ear-wigglers' as they are often found in the ears of grasses and

Green lacewings and brown lacewings are predators of aphids, both as larvae and as adults.

Gerard Cheshire

Judy Gallagher

Despite their appearance and their names, the scorpion fly (below) and the snake fly (right) are both perfectly harmless to humans.

Lynette Elliot

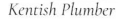

Kentish Plumber

The pincers of the earwig are used to catch prey, by folding the tail forwards, and to fend off predators. *G Boohne*

wiggle vigorously to escape when they are discovered. *Neuroptera* contains the lacewings, scorpion flies and snake flies.

There are various extremely small garden insects that often go unnoticed even though they may be present in large numbers. *Psocoptera* contains the barklice. *Thysanoptera* contains the thrips. *Collembola* contains the springtails. *Thysanura* contains the three-tailed bristletails. *Diplura* contains the two-tailed bristletails.

The springtail is an extremely small insect that uses a spring-loaded hair below it abdomen to jump from lone location to another. *Andy Murray*

CRUSTACEANS

In gardens the only terrestrial, or land-living, crustaceans are those known as slater woodlice (*Oniscus, Philoscia and Porcellio*) and pill woodlice (*Armadillidium*), which both belong to the order Isopoda. They are slightly different from one another, as pill woodlice can roll themselves into a pill-like sphere for protection from predators, whereas slater woodlice can only fold themselves. On the other hand, slater woodlice can secrete themselves in smaller spaces, because they have a flatter profile than pill woodlice. The term 'slater' is derived from the similarity of their body plates to a slate tile roof. Woodlice feed on decaying wood and plant matter. There is a species of spider – *Dysdera crocata* – that has evolved to specialize in hunting woodlice. It has articulating fangs that enable the spider to clasp the side of a woodlouse like a pair of tongs and then pierce its underbelly.

In ponds there are aquatic species similar to woodlice, called water slaters or hog lice (*Asellus*). In oxygenated streams there are freshwater shrimps (*Gammarus*). There are also microscopic crustaceans in ponds called copepods (*Cyclops* and *Diaptomus*) and water fleas (*Daphnia*). These animals form the foundation for the food chain in ponds and streams, along with other tiny organisms, such as hydras, protozoans, rotifers, water bears, bryozoans, sponges and amoebas.

The pill woodlouse *(left)* and the pill millipede *(right)* are very similar, but can be told apart by the tail end. *Gerard Cheshire*

The slater woodlouse cannot roll into a ball for protection, like the pill woodlouse, but it is better able to squeeze into tight spaces. *Gerard Cheshire*

Both the freshwater shrimp *(left)* and the water hog-louse *(right)* can be found in streams and ponds. The shrimp swims among waterweed, while the hog-louse walks along the bottom.

MILLIPEDES (Diplododa)

Some millipedes look rather like elongated woodlice. In fact, there are short millipedes too, called pill millipedes (*Glomeris*), which look virtually identical to pill woodlice. Upon closer inspection it is fairly easy to tell them apart, especially if both are side-by-side. Firstly, pill millipedes have two pairs of legs for each segment, while pill woodlice have one pair. Secondly, the tail end of the pill millipede comprises a single domed plate, while that of the pill woodlouse comprises several plates, because it is an ancestral tail that has been reduced in size by evolution. The pill millipede and the pill woodlouse are an example of convergent evolution: i.e. where unrelated species have

The snake millipede has a rounded profile and coils itself up to protect its head whenever it senses danger. *Nutmeg66*

The flat millipede is covered in armour plates that protect it from the jaws of predators, such a centipedes and spiders. *Gerard Cheshire*

The short and long soil millipedes are microscopic in size and are not closely related to other millipedes. *Andy Murray*

evolved to look and behave similarly because they have adapted to the same lifestyle.

Typical millipedes are long and thin, so that they can find their way through tiny gaps under stones and in soil, where they find shelter and food, which is dead plant matter, mosses and algae. Those with a rounded cross-section are known as snake millipedes, and those with a rectangular cross-section are known as flat-backed millipedes. In gardens they are commonly found beneath logs, under stones and in leaf litter, where they play an important role in recycling nutrients.

CENTIPEDES (Chilopoda)

Although centipedes look superficially similar to millipedes, they are quite different in terms of their lifestyle, for they are predators. They possess a pair of sensory poison claws, which come to the front of the head and function in much the same way as the pedipalps and fangs of a spider combined into one. In Britain there are no species dangerous to humans, as they are not large enough, but they are formidable hunters of other invertebrates. They have a flattened and elongated form to enable them to pursue their prey in small spaces, beneath stone, under leaf litter and in soil. In gardens there are two types of centipede: ribbon centipedes, which are very long and thin with pale colouring, and racer centipedes, which are relatively short but very fast on their feet and fulvous in colour.

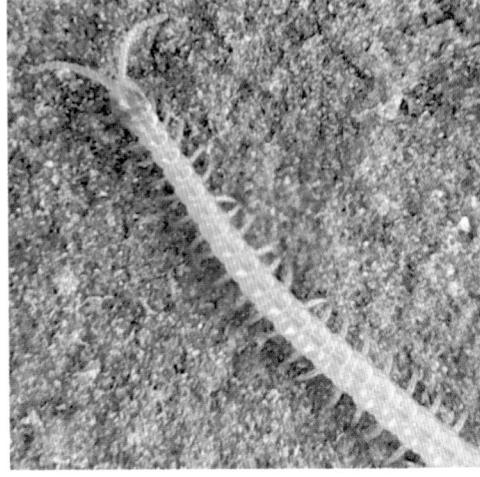

The thread centipede is very thin so that is can enter very small spaces in search of food. *Gerard Cheshire*

The front pair of legs of this centipede have evolved into fang-like appendages, which the animals uses to attack its prey with venom. *Bramble Jungle*

SYMPHYLANS

These creatures are sometime known as soil centipedes or false centipedes. They are very small and translucent which affords them camouflage. They live in soil as much as a metre deep, by using the tiny cracks created by expanding plant roots, as well as worm holes and so on. They generally eat decomposing plant matter, but will also eat the tender roots and root hairs of plants, which can be a problem when the symphylan population density is high. For the most part though, they play an important role in recycling nutrients in soil and providing food for other invertebrates. They are often abundant in compost heaps.

ARACHNIDS

In British gardens the arachnids fall into a number of orders: *Araneae* contains the spiders. *Opiliones* contains the harvestmen. *Acarina* contains the mites and ticks. *Pseudoscoriopnes* contains the false scorpions.

Spiders seem to trigger an instinctive primal fear in many humans, which is probably a behavioural vestige from their ancestors having lived in caves and rock shelters across Europe and other parts of the world in prehistory.

The garden spider *(left)* **and the crab spider** *(right)* **catch their prey in different ways, one with a web and the other by ambush.** *Gerard Cheshire*

As its name suggest, the woodlouse spider specializes in hunting woodlice. *Bathy Poreia*

The venomous bites of large cave spiders and cave centipedes (*Scutigera*) would have presented a genuine danger, so an evolved aversion reaction to long-legged and rapidly moving arthropods makes sense. All spiders are venomous as that is how they paralyze their prey, but there are no species dangerously venomous to humans in Britain. However, it is possible for people to develop necrosis, cellulitis and tetanus infections in spider bites or to suffer anaphylactic reactions to the venom, so it is best not to aggravate large spiders just in case they decide to defend themselves.

The most conspicuous spiders in gardens are those that belong to the *Argiopidae* family. They are the species that spin orb-webs for catching airborne insects. There are several species and they vary a great deal in size and shape. Also, the females are larger than the males, so they can be mistaken for different species. The most familiar orb spiders belong to the genus *Araneus*. The females have large rounded abdomens with cryptic patterning. Other garden spiders include sheet-web spiders, wolf spiders, jumping spiders and crab spiders.

Jumping spiders stalk their prey on the surfaces of walls, paths, tree trunks and so on. They have very good eyesight and pounce on their quarry by leaping surprising distances. Crab spiders hunt their prey by ambush. They sit on flowers with their limbs poised to grab visiting insects, which can be considerably larger than they are. Crab spiders have colour variations to help with camouflage.

The zebra spider is known as a jumping spider, because it stalks its prey and then leaps on it. *Gerard Cheshire*

Harvestmen are quite similar to spiders, but they have just one body part, whereas spiders have two. Their legs are relatively long and thin, and they are designed to detach should the harvestmen need to escape. They often have one, two, three or even four legs missing, yet still manage to walk. They feed by lowering their bodies onto their food, which is usually dead animal matter, so the long legs prevent them from getting soiled with sticky fluids. Having long legs is also very useful for walking through undergrowth and foliage. Some ground living species have shorter legs.

The most conspicuous mites seen in gardens are the bright red velvet mites (*Eutrombidium*) often seen swarming over rocks and walls on sunny days. Like spiders, they are predatory, but they feed on extremely small arthropods found in soil, due to their tiny size. Other mites include those that are sometimes

The velvet mite and false scorpion are tiny arachnids just, one or two millimetres long, that are often overlooked in our gardens. *Mick Talbot*

The tall and the short harvestman hunt for food by using their long legs to climb through the undergrowth. *Gerard Cheshire*

The deer tick attaches itself to the skin of mammals, where it then sucks their blood until fat and full.

seen attached to the bodies of large beetles and bumblebees, which are known as phoretic mites. They are not parasitic but use their hosts as a habitat and a method of transportation and dispersal.

Ticks feast on the blood of warm-blooded animals, including humans. As they feed on a succession of hosts as they grow, it means that ticks are often vectors of disease. The **deer tick** (*Ixodes*) is notorious for transmitting Lyme disease from birds and mammals to humans. Lyme disease varies greatly in its symptoms but can seriously affect the nervous system in some people, so it is always wise to remove ticks as quickly as possible.

False scorpions are so named because they have the pincers of a scorpion, but they have no tail, and therefore no sting. They are also extremely small, being just two or three millimetres in length. They are hardly ever noticed in gardens because they hunt for even smaller invertebrates in leaf litter, yet there are over twenty species in Britain.

MOLLUSCS

In British gardens, the *mollusc phylum* is represented by the gastropods: land snails, freshwater snails and land slugs. Slugs and snails are unusual in the animal world for being hermaphrodite; each animal being both male and female. However, this doesn't mean that they can reproduce asexually, or by parthenogenesis. They still pair-up and mate, so that each gives sperm to the other, and then both lay eggs fertilized by the other.

When garden snails mate, they attempt to fire calcareous barbed darts or harpoons into one another's flesh, thereby gaining a conveniently secure hold.

Mark Seton

Mark Robinson

J Maughn

Snails come in a variety of sizes, shapes and patterns, but their shells enable them to survive in relatively dry conditions.

Mating then takes place with the sexual organs. It has been discovered that the dart also introduces hormones into the other snail, via the slime, that increase sperm survival, so dart accuracy promotes both copulation success and gene survival and has therefore been favoured by natural selection. Having

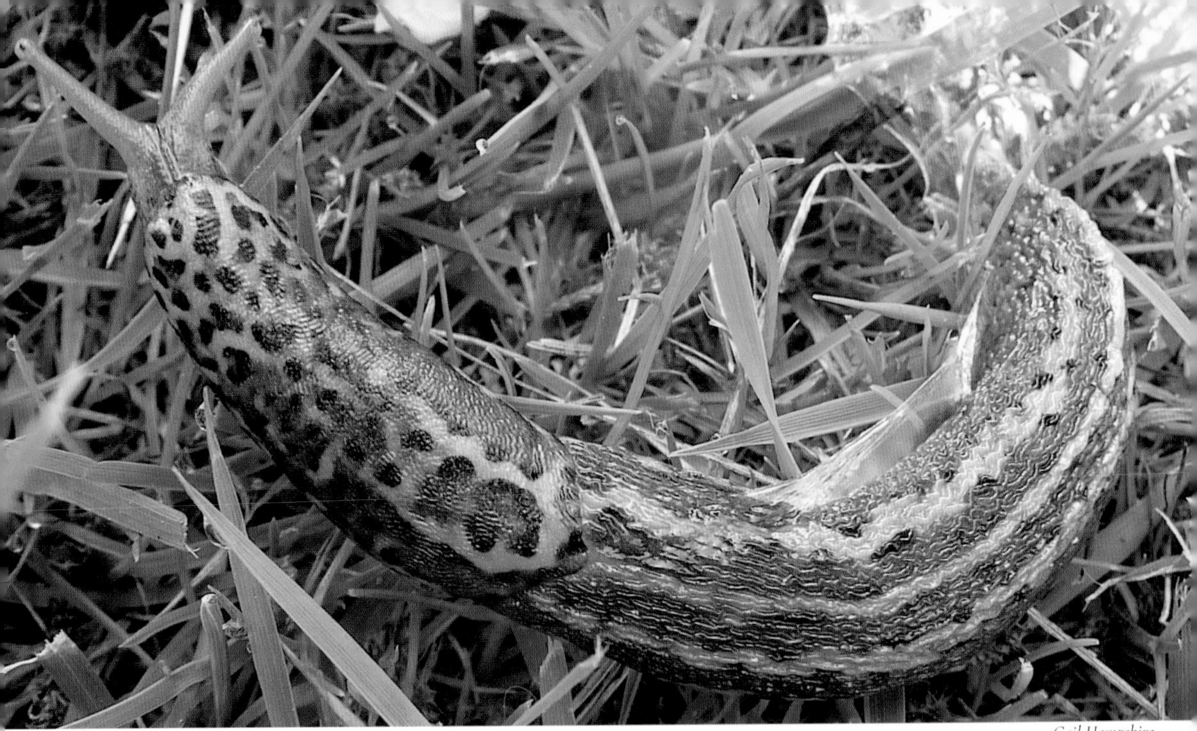

Gail Hampshire

Leopard ***(above)*** **and Orange-lipped slug** ***(below)*****. As they have no shells, slugs need to be careful about drying out and dying.**

Les Chatfield

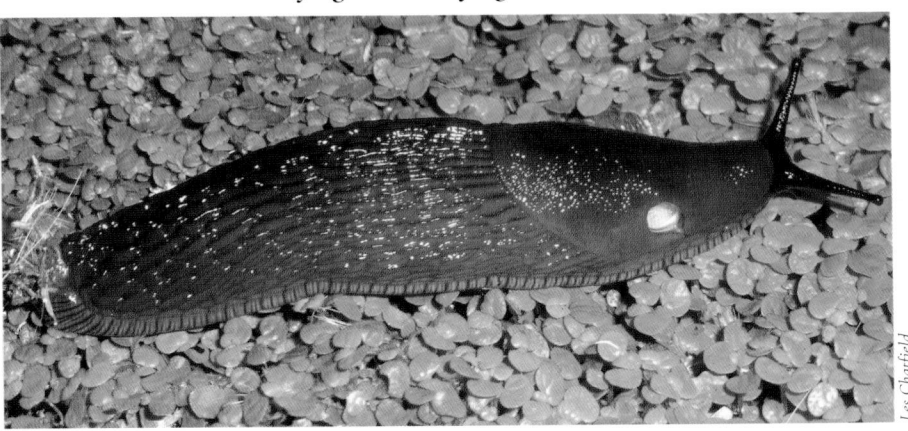

a shell brings both advantages and disadvantages, which is why slugs are just as successful as snails. A shell affords protection from predators and from desiccation, but it also hinders a snail's ability to fit into small spaces in order to hide or access potential food. As slugs have no shell they can squeeze and contort their way through narrow gaps to hide in damp places and to reach new resources. Anyone who has ever handled snails and slugs will know that slug slime is far more viscous and sticky that snail slime. This is an adaptation to avoid drying out. Slugs also contract in shape when at rest, to decrease their surface area for the same reason. Having a shell is clearly more advantageous in freshwater habitats than not having a shell, as freshwater slugs exist in some places in the world, but very rarely and not in Britain.

WORMS

The term 'worm' is used generically to describe many creatures that happen to have elongated bodies, such as woodworm, hornworm and glowworm. Here we are discussing animals that remain as worms in juvenile and adult form: i.e. earthworms, leeches, roundworms and flatworms.

Earthworms and leeches are known as annelid worms. They are segmented worms and the name 'annelid' derives from the Latin for 'small rings' in allusion to those segments. Earthworms are terrestrial and specialize in eating decomposing plant or vegetable matter. As they tunnel in the ground, they consume the soil and digest the organic material. They excrete the indigestible parts of the soil in the form of casts above ground. Earthworms also pull rotting leaves into their tunnels, so that they can feast on them whilst safely hidden from predators. They are prey for many higher animals, from songs birds and shrews to badgers and foxes. Earthworms move by using peristaltic waves to press many tiny outgrowths, called parapodia, against surfaces to gain traction. This method of locomotion doesn't work so well in water, so leeches have developed two different forms of locomotion: they can swim by undulating their bodies, and they can walk by 'looping' their bodies and using suckers. Leeches feed on the juices and blood of other animals. In the past it was believed that being bled by medicinal leeches (*Hirudo*) was a remedy for various ailments. These days, they are still used to improve the blood supply through body extremities following reconstructive surgery. Various species of leech can be found in garden ponds and streams, such as the fish leech (*Piscicola*), the duck leech (*Theromyzon*), the snail leech (*Glossiphonia*) and the predatory leeches (*Erpobdella & Haemopis*).

Earthworms and nematode worms both live in garden soil, but earthworms are ginats in comparison with nematodes.

Peter Hartl   *Christophe Quintin*

Melissa McMasters

Pond leeches *(above)* and fish leeches *(below)* are found in ponds and slow
moving streams and canals.

Mark Robinson

Nematode worms are very small transparent non-segmented worms that
live in soil and play a vital role in nutrient recycling. In soil with plenty of
organic matter and compost heaps, these worms can number in their millions
per cubic metre, yet they are seldom noticed because they are all but invisible
to the human eye.

Flatworms, otherwise known as planaria, live in ponds and are very
unusual in having no gut. Instead of eating, they absorb nutrients through
the surface of their bodies. This is why they have flat bodies, to optimize their
surface area to volume ratio. They absorb oxygen from the water in the same
way.

PLANTS

There are, of course, many hundreds of species of plant native to British gardens. It would be impracticable to list them all, so here we discuss them in botanical groups: the broad divisions of the flora are as follows: algae (charophytes), liverworts (marchantiophytes), mosses (bryophytes), horsetails and ferns (pteridophytes), conifers (gymnosperms), flowering plants (angiosperms). Fungi, such as mushrooms, toadstools, yeasts, slimes and moulds, are similar to primitive plants, while lichens are a combination of algal plant and fungus in symbiotic partnership.

ALGAE

In freshwater habitats, algae range in complexity from the microscopic single-celled plants that give pond water its green hue, to more complex structures known as chara, or stoneworts. They are the most basic of plants, as they don't have cells specialized for different purposes.

LIVERWORTS

Sometimes known as hepatics, the liverworts are simple semi-aquatic plants that live at the margins of freshwater. They reproduce by creating spores, which have the ability to survive if the habitat becomes too dry for the plants to live. The spores then grow into new plants when dampness returns, or if they find their way to new damp places.

MOSSES

The mosses are also simple plants, but they have the ability to live on land, away from water. They grow when water is available and become dormant when conditions lead to desiccation: i.e. they aestivate. They release spores from capsules attached to stems, so that they stand a good chance of dispersal. In gardens, mosses can be found growing on walls, roof tiles, tree trunks and amongst the grass of lawns. There are many species and they typically form cushions or mats of feathery stems.

HORSETAILS AND FERNS

These plants also produce spores, but they also have well-developed root systems, so they don't need to fix themselves to other objects. Instead they are able to take root and colonize soils. As a result, these were the first plants to spread across the land and they dominated earth until the eventual evolution of seed producing plants. In gardens, various horsetail and ferns species can become established. Some grow as solitary plants and others spread invasively, so they often need to be controlled to ensure that they don't force out other plants.

CONIFERS

The term 'gymnosperm' derives from the Latin for 'naked seed', as these plants produce seeds that are not enclosed by a husk or shell. Instead they develop within a cone and them become exposed as the cone opens. Unlike spores, seeds carry food for the embryo, so that it is more likely to survive and develop into a new plant. However, they are more costly to produce than spores and fewer can be produced, so there is a trade-off. The most familiar of these plants are pines, larches, spruces, hemlocks, cypresses, cedars, firs and junipers. They typically have needle-like leaves.

FLOWERING PLANTS.

The term 'angiosperm' derives from the Latin for 'enclosed seed' as these plants protect their seeds within a husk or a shell. In addition, they are typically developed within a fruit, a drupe or a berry, so that animals are attracted and help to disperse the seeds. In the case of nuts, acorns, and chestnuts, the incentive is inside the seed, so a certain number are sacrificed in order that a few find their way to suitable new locations. In some cases, the seeds are simply produced en masse, as with grasses and thistles, and often equipped with ways of allowing the wind to disseminate them. The flowering plants are a diverse group of plants. They include deciduous and evergreen broadleaf trees, such as oaks, hornbeams, beeches, limes, hollies, maples, chestnuts, ashes, privets, birches, fruit-trees, walnuts and willows. They also include the flowering herbaceous and woody plants, such as the daisy family, the mint family, the rose family, the umbellifer family, the cabbage family, the buttercup family, the campion family, the geranium family, the orchid family, the clover family, the saxifrage family, the heather family, the spurge family, the lily family, the iris family, the onion family and many more besides. In addition, there are the grasses, the sedges and the rushes. These plants range in size from tiny meadow and ruderal herbs to enormous trees, so they form the basis of the flora in most gardens. They have evolved alongside the mammals, birds, reptiles, amphibians, fish and invertebrates, so there is complex network of interrelationships. In other words, both the fauna and flora are essentials parts of the natural ecosystem, so a healthy garden is one that has a good mix of both.

FUNGI AND LICHENS

Fungi are not plants and they are not animals either. They fall somewhere between the two. They include toadstools, mushrooms, puffballs, moulds, yeasts and slimes. The fungi that we notice in our gardens are the fruiting bodies of the organisms, which develop in order to release and distribute spores. The actual organism is unseen, as it comprises a network of filaments, called hyphae, in the soil or in rotting wood, called the mycelium. Fungi are another essential part of the ecosystem, as they play an important role in recycling organic matter and they also assist many plants in their

access to vital nutrients by combining with their root systems. This is a form of symbiosis, which is where two organisms benefit from their close association.

Lichens take symbiosis one stage further, by combining to create a single organism. So, a lichen is a fungus (*Lecanoromycetes*) with a colony of algae (*Trebouxia*) living inside it, so that each provides the other with resources. The fungus provides a fixed and safe environment for the algae and it also absorbs water and nutrients from the surroundings. The algae return the favour by photosynthesizing energy for the fungus. Thus, both types of organism are able to survive in the most unlikely places in gardens, such as the surface of tree trunks, on rocks, on bricks, on pavers and on roof tiles.

Lichens acquire nutrients from the surface on which they grow, which often contains minerals and organic compounds from invertebrate and bird excreta. They also acquire nutrients from rainwater, so they are very sensitive to pollutants such as dissolved sulphur-dioxide and carbon-dioxide, which cause 'acid rain'. This makes them useful indicators of air quality in towns and cities. Litmus, which is familiar to school children as an indicator of acidity in science classes, is extracted from lichens, as the organisms actually change colour according to air purity. Red-brown indicates low pH value (acidity) and blue-green indicates high pH value (alkalinity).

Moulds, yeasts and slimes are more primitive fungi that can also be found commonly in gardens, on rotting fruit and logs. Yeasts produce alcohol when they grow in the fruit, so animals that consume the juices then become intoxicated. This can include wasps, butterflies, birds and deer. Their behaviour changes, so that they become disorientated, clumsy and slower in their reactions.